GATHERED IN THE SPIRIT

Cover illustration: Fourth meetinghouse of the First Church in Cambridge. Drawing by Perry K. Neubauer after a lithograph published in Lectures on the History of the First Church in Cambridge *by Alexander McKenzie, Boston, Mass.: Congregational Publishing Society, 1873.*

GATHERED IN THE SPIRIT

Beginnings of the First Church in Cambridge

SUSAN DRINKER MORAN

UNITED CHURCH PRESS
Cleveland, Ohio

United Church Press, Cleveland, Ohio 44115
© 1995 by Susan Drinker Moran

Biblical quotations are from the New Revised Standard Version of the Bible,
© 1989 by the Division of Christian Education of the National Council of the
Churches of Christ in the U.S.A., and are used by permission

Printed in the United States of America on acid-free paper

00 99 98 97 96 95   5 4 3 2 1

Library of Congress Cataloging-in-Publication Data

Moran, Susan Drinker, 1927–
    Gathered in the Spirit : beginnings of the First Church in Cambridge / Susan
Drinker Moran.
        p.   cm.
    Includes bibliographical references and index.
    ISBN 0-8298-1069-2 (alk. paper)
    1. First Church (Cambridge, Mass.)—History.   2. Cambridge (Mass.)—
Church history.   I. Title.
BX9886.Z7C3245   1995
285.8'7444—dc20   95-16998
                                                                    CIP

For my father and mother,
Philip Drinker and Susan Aldrich Drinker

CONTENTS

FOREWORD

When we consider that the Salem witch hysteria of 1692 may be the most widely remembered episode of pre-Revolutionary New England—rivaled only by Thanksgiving traditions descended from the Pilgrims of Plymouth—or that Nathaniel Hawthorne's *The Scarlet Letter* is the most frequently read book about early American Puritans, we may gain some sense of both historical ignorance and the need for a better grasp of formative influences in the European settlement of North America.

Begun as lectures to a Christian congregation that traces its origins to the beginning of worship in Cambridge in 1632, these essays bring to the reader a sense of the present relevance of the early church history of New England. In conveying the piety and passion of early settlers, they evoke our feelings as well.

You may wonder about the foibles or the wisdom of the founders described here, their dedication, and their construction of a new society. But you will find unmistakable in this account their fervent love for God and their urgent quest to fashion a righteous commonwealth. For all the changes and vagaries of intervening time, their heritage remains in Cambridge. People still gather each sabbath in this Massachusetts town with the humble confidence that Christ is with them and that they will be led by the Spirit.

In these chapters Susan Moran takes us past the stereotypes of stern Calvinism and rigid dogmatism to the devotion and vision of Thomas Hooker, the first pastor in Cambridge, who taught his congregation to pray:

Good Lord, let thy servant now hear a seasonable word. Quicken these dead bones here before thee. Speak home to my conscience, wound my corruptions, slay these sins that are too hard for me, let no iniquity prevail over thy poor servant, but let Jesus Christ be all in all to and in me. Take this heart of mine, and frame it, and alter it, and mold it, and melt it. Work thine own will in me, fashion me to thy kingdom of grace here that I may partake of thy kingdom of glory hereafter.[1]

Allen Happe
Fifteenth Pastor of the First Church in Cambridge

PREFACE

The chapters in this volume have been adapted from a series of lectures delivered at the First Church in Cambridge, Congregational, United Church of Christ, between 1982 and 1986, in preparation for and in celebration of the three-hundred-fiftieth anniversary of the gathering of the church. The story of the church's beginning is, however, of general interest because of its importance in the history of early New England and in the development of the congregational tradition. For this reason, a more formal presentation of the material seemed appropriate.

The church was founded by two overlapping waves of English Puritan immigrants who settled three years apart in the village originally called Newtown, on the banks of the Charles River. In the first migration came Thomas Hooker who, together with his younger colleague, Samuel Stone, arrived in Newtown in 1633. They were to become the pastor and teacher, respectively, of the church that had been gathered there one year earlier by a band of Hooker's English followers from Essex. In the autumn of 1635 Thomas Shepard arrived in Newtown with a group of his own devoted followers brought together out of Essex, Yorkshire, and Northumberland. He was installed as pastor in February in anticipation of Hooker's springtime departure for Hartford, Connecticut, where he and most of his congregation would relocate their church. The church founded by Hooker and Shepard, like the other early New England churches, lay at the heart of the culture, spreading its influence deeply and widely into the social, educational, political, and economic fabric of the society. In Newtown, in particular, during the years between the arrival of Hooker and Stone and the death of Shepard in 1649 events took place that were of importance for the church, for the community, and ultimately even for the future nation. In 1636 Harvard College was founded, and two years later Newtown became Cambridge. In 1637 Anne Hutchinson, the controversial religious leader from Boston, was tried in the Newtown meetinghouse and eventually banished, with enormous consequences for the New England churches and their society. In 1648 the Cambridge Platform of Church Discipline—the earliest formulation of Congregational polity and discipline—was devised and promulgated. Although unique in their specifics and in the personalities that moved through them and propelled them, these events took place in a context that was not unique. The English background in which they were rooted, the New English circumstances that gave rise to them, and the consequences they produced give the history of the First Church in Cambridge a significance far beyond its modest beginnings.

My hope in designing these lectures was to bring to life in concrete and human terms the faith of the men and women who first worshipped in Cambridge. As a guide in that endeavor, some basic questions about the lives of these early New Englanders were formulated. What was it about their faith and their life together that so deeply satisfied their spiritual and emotional needs? What in their theology so kindled their imaginations? What was it that focused their lives in sustained commitment? By keeping these questions in mind while exploring the background and early history of the First Church in Cambridge, I hoped that we might come closer to discovering who these men and women really were.

I chose to focus my story on the nature and history of the church as "gathered" because the gathered church as it was conceived and eventually brought into being as an institution expressed the essence of Puritan sensibility and Puritan thought, and because the ideal has persisted as a creative element in the governance and spirituality of the church in Cambridge as well as in other churches in the congregational tradition and beyond. Chapter 1 begins the narrative with an introduction to the idea of the gathered church as it emerged in late sixteenth and early seventeenth century England, which is followed by a discussion of its early development in England and in the Massachusetts Bay Colony. Chapter 2 explores the English roots of the faith of the two founders of the church in Cambridge, and chapter 3 describes their painful decision to emigrate. Chapter 4 sees the hopes of Hooker and Shepard and their companies of believers brought to fruition in the village of Newtown. The story concludes in the epilogue with a look at the forces that were beginning to adulterate the purity of the gathered church as it had been conceived by Hooker and Shepard.

Since the sources from which I have quoted are varied and were, therefore, printed according to a variety of editorial principles, I have standardized all quotations following the procedure of Michael McGiffert in his *God's Plot: Puritan Spirituality in Thomas Shepard's Cambridge*, from which I have quoted extensively. Thus spelling, punctuation, and capitalization have all been modernized except in the case of titles, and italics have been omitted. Editorial interpolations have been placed within brackets.

It should be noted that it is the editorial policy of United Church Press to require, in all references to the personhood of God, in every context, the use of inclusive language. Quoted material is excepted.

ACKNOWLEDGMENTS

My interest in the life and ministry of Thomas Shepard in England and New England began many years ago. During a six-month stay in England I was able to explore the country where he lived and travel the road that he had traveled. In the course of that journey, I was made welcome in the towns and churches important to his development, especially by the Reverend A. S. J. Holden, Vicar of St. Andrew's Church in Earls Colne, Essex, and by the late R. C. Chapman of Abthorp, Northamptonshire, who shared his detailed knowledge of the Shepard family with me. P. I. King and Arthur Searle, archivists of the Northamptonshire Record Office and the Essex Record Office, gave me expert and generous guidance through the parish registers, wills, and ecclesiastical court records in their care. Closer to home, when I had begun to focus my attention more directly on the early history of the first church in Cambridge, I was much helped by the staff of the Houghton Library at Harvard University. In particular, I am grateful to Rodney Dennis, whose expertise in Church Latin and in the intricacies of the seventeenth-century script helped me to understand English church records and to learn to decipher Shepard's handwriting. Most recently, Katie Sasser, of the Hawthorne-Longfellow Library at Bowdoin College, has been infinitely patient and resourceful in answering bibliographical questions.

Among my associates at the First Church in Cambridge, I especially want to thank Alice Goodwin-Brown for encouraging me to begin; Scott Magoon for his lively interest, his humor, and his merciless prodding; and Allen Happe, most of all. He has given me unflagging, enthusiastic support at every stage, and in the course of many long conversations has led me to new insights from his own study of Cambridge church history.

The generosity of the readers who have given their time so freely is a source of absolute wonder to me. Catherine F. Garlid, Scott Magoon, and Patricia H. Rodgers have helped as general readers who have offered perceptive criticism, each from a different perspective. Allen Happe, David Ferry, and especially Anne Ferry and Jo Ann Hackett have given me thoughtful and meticulous professional advice which has significantly shaped these chapters. Over many years, George H. Williams has greatly deepened and widened my understanding of Reformation history. In spite of serious illness, he has read my manuscript a second time with undiminished interest and critical candor. My debt to him is enormous. At a difficult juncture, the encouragement and advice of Michael McGiffert gave me new spirit and helpful direction. A technical crisis was expertly resolved by Jo Ann Hackett and John Huehnergard, who retrieved my lost footnotes out of the mysterious labyrinth of my computer. Three artists have made this a richer and livelier book than it could otherwise have been. Stephen Ferry, Julia C. Drinker, and especially Perry K. Neubauer have offered me their talents and expertise in a fashion that will be immediately evident to the reader. William L. Moran is in a special category as reader and rereader, supporter, objective and rigorous critic, artistic adviser, beloved husband, and friend. Always warmly available to talk, he has helped me with issues great and small, from faulty grammar and errant style, to weighty theological matters. I am grateful to him, most of all.

INTRODUCTION

The life and thought of Thomas Hooker (1586–1647), minister in Newtown/Cambridge of the Massachusetts Bay Colony, and of his successor, Thomas Shepard (1605–1649), are of great interest in their own right and also because both these pastoral leaders of settlers were representative thinkers of the first New England generation of Puritans. While recounting the lives of these first two pastors in Cambridge, Susan Drinker Moran evokes the stirring beginnings of New England as a whole. Hooker himself becomes, for example, the founder of another Puritan commonwealth.

Scarcely arrived in the Bay Colony, Thomas Hooker and his company separated from it with all of their goods and gear and, after a six-day trek through the primeval forest, as an intact gathered congregation, founded a new colony, Connecticut, with its emerging capital, Hartford. In the first years of the emigration from old England, this was a Congregational colony jurisdictionally separate by charter from that of New Haven (only later to coalesce as one). The two ministerial leaders and theologians, Thomas Hooker and Thomas Shepard, looming large in the ensuing account, were among the handful of clerical thinkers—alongside the elected Puritan governors and other magistrates—who laid the foundation of New England polity and who shaped the theology and the moral standards of the brave enterprise. Far beyond their original intentions and expectations, this enterprise would become a new kind of community of faith and political conviction in the first two generations in New England.

At the time of the ensuing account, Plymouth Colony of the Pilgrims was also a wholly independent religio-political jurisdiction. From the outset in 1620, the Pilgrims to the south of the Massachusetts Bay Colony had maintained a different Congregational polity from that of the Bay Colony (although they would later be more or less forcibly joined with it). The Pilgrims displayed a few more features of a gathered (voluntarist) church, although, like the Puritans, they continued to practice infant baptism of their offspring. In being less stringent in their territorial congregational regimen than the Bay colonists, the Plymouth settlers were closer to the Baptists, like Roger Williams, in his programmatic separation of church and state in Rhode Island. (However, the founder of Rhode Island was only transitionally a Baptist for a scant year [1639], whereupon he called himself simply a "seeker.") It may be remarked in passing, to round out our suggestion that polity was in flux in the first two generations in New England, that the baptism of adult believers eventually would be adopted by another major Puritan divine, Henry Dunster, the learned builder of Harvard College in Cambridge. In 1655 Dunster would be obliged to seek refuge over the line in Plymouth Colony as a convert to believers' baptism as the proper qualification for membership in the true (believers') church/congregation.

Although the original and fervent desire of the Bay colonists and of the urban Congregational colonists was to assist strategically from afar in the reformation of the Reformation in England, history shows that they shaped a quite new modality of Reformed Christendom for a large part of the British North America yet to be. With an unforeseen massive impact on the eventually pan-Protestant traits of the new nation to emerge, extending far beyond the borders of even their rounded out New England, the first settlers of Boston Bay, Connecticut, and New Haven were still thinking through the consequences of their mighty acts in their expansion in the old England and the new. Hooker and Shepard, their fellow divines, the founding magistrates, and the early devout settlers under them thought of themselves as setting up the model of a fully Reformed England, which scarcely two decades later would indeed endure civil and confessional strife over polity (1642–

1646) forever staining with blood the warp and woof of English society. At the same time these congregational conquistadores were in fact shaping a distinctively new form of pietistic sectarian and yet territorial (ecclesiastical) Christianity, which was destined to mold, to endow with new institutions, and to suffuse with new social expectations and energies the Christianity of wide stretches of the New World—far beyond the settlement of what would become New England.

In brief, these English colonists, Shepard and Hooker among them, thought through and established a new Christian polity, without historic precedent in Europe: with contiguous but not overlapping territorial congregations (eventually parishes with their nuclear believers' churches), independent of each other but together supportive of magistrates of the same or similar convictions and religio-political presuppositions. Theirs was a radically reconceived neo-Anglican Congregationalism—that is, contiguous Congregationalism.

The core of these communities, distinctive of this New World territorial Congregationalism, was innovatingly simple and strenuous. It was sustained by the social will to preserve the Anglican heritage of an established church, but now with two strands, never quite fully braided. The first of these strands was the church/congregation (eventually the parish-church) of any given colonial territory, under uniformly Christian law, as substantially undergirded by the Old Testament; it was understood to be established for the upkeep of the ministry and magistracy and for the nurture of children in the covenant over the whole territorial population—infants, slaves, and subdued indigenous peoples included. Second, within this aggregation of independent congregations (each calling and salarying its own minister as "public teacher"), existed what could be described as the true church of the experientially qualified full members, communicant members, or communing believers. The congregation as a whole thus acted in the twofold role of temporal and religious body.

The true believers in Cambridge, whom we will take as our example, were known only to God and theoretically were not always clearly distinguishable from the nominal believers in the same town.

The theological difference was in salvation by faith alone, as manifest in a saving experience, which when recounted before members of the church assembled apart, qualified the Puritan in Cambridge or else-where to be admitted to the very simple but solemn quarterly commu-nion through the Lord's Supper. All those required to attend the weekly services of the public teacher on the Sabbath presumably looked forward with intense longing to such a qualifying experience. In the meantime inhabitants without such an experience could neither participate in communion nor vote in the town and colony elections.

The eventual core of each town and its parish—namely, the church of true believers, (the chosen saints)—was the company of those re-born or regenerated by God's grace, which was perceptible to them-selves alone in their quickened faith. These were understood by the community at large to be known to God from eternity and assigned their blessed destiny in their primordial election known to each saint but only in his or her personal experience of salvation by faith alone.

Never before in the history of Christianity were the demands on prospective recruits into the *militia Christi* so exacting, except for the discipline imposed by the medieval church and its orders upon postu-lants in several monastic congregations. The ecclesiology of the New England Puritans of the classical normative period could best be char-acterized as *connubial coenobitism* (conjugal monasticism), the living together of devout disciples and their still-to-be-redeemed offspring, servants, and transients, all in close mutual watch over and care for the other.

All this is to describe the formalization of—and indeed formuliza-tion of—the polity and theology of the Congregational colonies a gen-eration after the principal figures of the book before us had thought through the theological consequences and the ecclesial implications of their original vision. But it is helpful to have some sense of how the new religio-political mix will soon harden after being poured into the expectant hearts by the Holy Spirit and made manifest to others, al-ready communicants in the intimate testimony of converts in the bo-som of the church. The following vivid biographical accounts help us to grasp the meaning of pioneer experiential and established Congregationalism.

Susan Drinker Moran deftly tells the story of some of the shapers of New England, including the views of one highly articulate female critic among these, Anne Hutchinson, as they thought through and expressed their faith before some of the foregoing generalizations were entirely clear even to the participants.

George H. Williams
Hollis Professor of Divinity, Emeritus
Harvard University

THE GATHERED CHURCH IN
ENGLAND AND NEW ENGLAND

Secret Beginnings in England

Writing from Newgate Prison in 1572, a distinguished Puritan divine named John Field defined a gathered church in words that expressed the intent of his contemporaries. The church, he wrote, is

> a company or congregation of the faithful called and gathered out
> of the world by the preaching of the gospel, who following and
> embracing true religion, do in one unity and spirit strengthen and
> comfort one another, daily growing and increasing in true faith,
> framing their lives, government, orders and ceremonies according
> to the word of God. [1]

The important phrase here is "called and gathered out of the world." Members of the true church, according to Field, were not simply born into it. Rather, as a seventeenth-century covenant from the first years in New England tells us, they were gathered in the Spirit out of the world into an intimate fellowship "in mutual love and respect each to other, so near as God shall give us grace."[2] It is the early development of their ideal church in England, its transplantation to New England, and its particular manifestation in Cambridge that form the content of these chapters.

In order to discover the reason for the power of the ideal among both the friends and the foes of the incipient church, it will be helpful to begin with a look at the intellectual and institutional context from which it emerged. We must make a cautious attempt to reconstruct something of the frame of reference and habits of thought of most Protestant English men and women in the late sixteenth and early seventeenth centuries, whether they were conforming members of the Church of England or Puritans.

Although they may not have experienced their world as a more disorderly or frightening one than we do our own, their perception of the sources of disorder and the kinds of philosophy and theology that were marshaled to make their lives more manageable and to give them meaning were very different. Renaissance men and women inhabited a world in which forces that we would today separate into natural and supernatural were mingled without distinction, in which portents and wonders abounded. Ghostly appearances, the sinister motions of witches, "monster" births, hailstorms and earthquakes, all had potentially fearful meaning and added an increased sense of vulnerability to the people's already vivid awareness of the closeness of disease, death, and natural disaster. In this life it sometimes seemed that "nothing was secure, . . . no appearance of security could hide the mystery beneath."[3]

Mingled with these disorderly images and fears inherited from antiquity and medieval lore and learning was a multilayered response, also largely inherited, that was given a new focus in the late sixteenth century by the pervasive influence in England of the continental Reformed theology of Ulrich Zwingli, Martin Bucer, and of John Calvin in particular. For many this focus gave meaning to disorder and direction to life, especially for those who heard the call to New England.

Perhaps the most vital element in this response was what one scholar has called "the predestinarian consensus."[4] Reformed theologians of all stripes agreed on this tenet, which is embedded in much English theological discourse of the period and which deeply engaged the imagination of the leaders of the migration to New England and their parishioners. Primary, in their minds, was the awful might of a highly patriarchal God, a Creator and Father who fashioned the universe to the end that the Godhead should be glorified by all creation, and whose consistent purpose directed every event. There could be no chance occurrence. "God attends to the government of particular events. . . . They all proceed from his determinate counsel in such manner that there can be no such thing as a fortuitous contingence," said John Calvin, quelling the fear of disorder.[5] If all that happens to human or beast or oak or fading flower is ordered by God's intent and plan, and if an afterlife in either heaven or hell is predestined, then seemingly random and perhaps frightening events readily become endowed with purpose and meaning. If one's place in the ancient hierarchical structure of society—be it knight or yeoman or goodwife—has been ordained by God, then willing obedience becomes acquiescence to God's will.

In order that divine power might be made more fully manifest and a divine nature both just and merciful be revealed, God conceived and then unfolded the drama of salvation. It began when God placed two newly formed human creatures in the Garden of Eden and explained to them the conditions under which they were henceforth to live there. Adam and Eve were given a law that was to be perfectly obeyed. In return for obedience they were to receive eternal life and face to face communion with God. Reformed theologians of the late sixteenth century called this promise made by God to Adam and Eve and their compliance with it the covenant of works. When the law was broken, Adam and Eve and all of their descendants were condemned to eternal separation from God. Human nature was transformed from innocence to corruption; the daily round of life, from blissful idleness to harshness and toil; the future, from eternal life with God to eternal isolation and fiery damnation. Thus was God's justice satisfied.

However, this just God was also merciful, unwilling to abandon humankind completely. Accordingly, a new dispensation was revealed through which justice could be satisfied and at the same time divine mercy be made manifest. Jesus, the only Son of God, was offered as a sacrifice to be the Christ who would come to earth and who would die in payment for human sin. Through death Jesus atoned for that sin and made salvation possible for those who were given the grace to believe in him. When the men and women who had been predestined by God to be saved were given the grace to believe, the righteousness of the Christ was imputed to them without regard to any good works. They were, in other words, accepted by God as if they truly *were* righteous. They were justified (made just) by their faith alone and became, once again, reconciled to God. In a new covenant, a covenant of grace, God promised unconditionally to be bound in love, to shelter forever those who had been chosen.[6] At the same time that God blessed the elect with forgiveness and mercy, however, Reformed preachers taught that divine justice had been exercised in the damnation of the others, the reprobate. Theirs was a damnation the saints had also deserved but were saved from by free grace.

This stark theology, which fueled a revolution in England and filled the minds and hearts of the leaders of a great migration to the New World, is difficult for us to comprehend with sympathy, especially in its emphasis on an election to reprobation or to glory that had been predestined without regard to human behavior. It may also have been a difficult as well as frightening theology for many of our forebears. For others it was a doctrine of inspiration and unspeakable comfort. It could mean release from the struggle to win divine favor by striving unceasingly to please God, release from a self-centered and agitated preoccupation with one's own salvation. One could affirm one's destiny and get on with doing God's will for God's sake, acting out of love for the Creator and in dependence on God's almighty power and enduring goodness. This was the way John Cotton of Boston, Lincolnshire, and later of Boston in Massachusetts Bay, felt. Cotton, a close student of Calvin, when asked why he studied so late at night, is said to have replied: "I like to sweeten my mouth with a piece of Calvin before I sleep."[7]

Until well into the seventeenth century this Reformed consensus held sway over much of the Church of England, encompassing under its two archbishops a considerable variety of doctrinal emphases. For the Puritans within the consensus, the sources of discontent with the established church were much less doctrinal than institutional. The institution of the church, many people felt, was no longer responding adequately to its calling. Puritanism was a movement of revival within the Church of England. It was a summons to clergy and laity alike to breathe new life into a decaying institution and to purify its liturgy in the image of what its leaders saw as the true church of early Christianity.

Much of the structure of the English medieval church had remained intact after the separation from Rome, but a good deal of the lifeblood had gone out of it. The Roman church of the Middle Ages had been the matrix of the lives of all western Christians. It had nurtured its parishioners, given their lives meaning, and informed their choices from the beginning to the end of their lives. In so doing it had commanded their unquestioned allegiance. The economic, political, and ecclesiastical resources the medieval church possessed had made possible the consistent and largely efficient performance of these obligations.

The nationalization of the church seriously unsettled the allegiance of many ordinary, believing Christians and also increasingly sapped the vitality and integrity of the institution. The chaotic swings in ecclesiastical polity and in theology which took place in the space of a single lifetime in post-Reformation England may have had little effect on masses of poorly educated parishioners who were far from the sources of power, but they sorely tried the understanding and commitment of many earnest churchgoers who were dragged along behind. The traumatic break with Rome under Henry VIII was followed, under his young son Edward VI, by a significant theological shift toward Reformed doctrine. Then the pendulum swung back again to Rome, under Mary Tudor, and back once more to a national church, under Elizabeth I, in what proved to be an enduring compromise. Such demands on the allegiance of those English men and women who were looking for nothing more than spiritual guidance and perhaps social stability must have been highly confusing, if not seriously disorienting.

There were signs also of real deterioration in the institutional church. The quality of the higher clergy was uneven, partly as a result of its dependence on the crown. Appointed by the state, the clergy's allegiance was inevitably divided, and the function of preaching frequently became as much to uphold the crown as to point the way to salvation. The lower clergy, too, suffered from secular influences as a result of nationalization. As the appointees of careless if not unscrupulous landlords, they often lived in poverty, were poorly educated, and frequently either unable or unwilling to preach.

In an age in which the leaders of society demanded and depended upon the enforcement of strict standards to keep an ignorant and unruly populace in order, a decline in effective church discipline was a further source of discontent among critics of the Church of England. After the Reformation the ecclesiastical courts, which had been administered by the Roman Catholic church, continued under new management to perform their accustomed function, with the addition of the Court of High Commission as highest authority. Christians had little quarrel with this system: all agreed that "adultery, whoredom, incest, drunkenness, swearing, ribaldry, usury," and other "uncleanness and wickedness of life" must be punished.[8] Some of them, however, deplored the manner in which church discipline was administered. The courts were impersonal and often far from the parish where the offense had been committed. Therefore, court officials had little understanding of either the reported transgression or the transgressor. Worse still was a creeping corruption in court practices. Penance might be commuted to money payments for those who could afford it. Excommunication could be used for political purposes. Most offensive of all, preaching ministers who expressed dissatisfaction with the inadequacy of the system were suspended by local courts and sometimes tried by the Court of High Commission.

Criticism of the Church of England mounted, and programs designed to reform and "purify" the Church began to be formulated both by clergy and by a number of well-educated and concerned lay people. These Puritans, as they were soon derisively known, called for a church that would inflame hearts, turn lives around, offer comfort to the weary and sorrowful, and give real direction to life. They wanted to counter apathy, corruption, and disorganization with enthusiasm, rectitude, and efficiency. Some of these critics began to focus their hopes for change in the church on the vision of a community of faith gathered in the Spirit and guided by a pastor who would be a dedicated preacher of the Word. Such a community, they believed, could truly make known the urgency of the gospel and bring its message into being in the lives of men and women all over England.

The doctrine that inspired the vision of the gathered church and underlay its eventual creation was Pauline, based on the Apostle's conception of the church as the spiritual body of Christ, which "joined and knit together by every ligament with which it is equipped, as each part is working properly, promotes the body's growth in building itself up in love" (Eph. 4:16). This doctrine is, of course, a formative ideal for all Christian communities. For certain Puritans, however, it was central. It was their primary concern. Since they interpreted it very concretely, all aspects of their church sprang from it: church government, liturgy, and discipline.

To these Puritans a spiritual body meant a holy community made up of men and women who had been touched by the Spirit and who, as they felt the hand of God upon them, were intuitively drawn together by the shared experience. They would form a community as closely knit as was possible for Christians on earth, which would inspire in them a commitment expressed in a two-dimensional covenant, binding them to God and to one another. This covenanted fellowship would then call and ordain a minister to be its pastor. Where there was no covenant, there could be no church; and where there was no congregational call, there could be no pastor.

The attitude of these Puritans toward ritual and liturgy was rooted in their ideal of the holy community. Only those ceremonies and that liturgy which contributed to the edification or building up of the spiritual body were acceptable. Church of England leaders and Puritans, both standing firmly in the Reformed tradition, agreed that ceremonies in themselves were unimportant to God. Those who spoke for the Church of England believed, however, that the choice of ritual and liturgy should be guided by tradition and by what was aesthetically pleasing. Not so the Puritans. For them no ceremony or liturgy that might be misinterpreted by ignorant and superstitious people and thereby become a source of idolatry could be used in worship. Rituals forbidden on this principal included sealing the bond of marriage with a ring, making the sign of the cross in baptism, and bowing at the name of Jesus. Kneeling to receive the Lord's Supper was unacceptable because it might appear to the ignorant to be worship of a "breaden God." The Puritans discouraged set prayers because they felt that spontaneity better expressed the inspiration of the Spirit and they feared that rote prayers might be used in a superstitious fashion. In the same way, they encouraged varied congregational responses instead of structured litanies, which they felt were like "the tossing to and fro of tennis balls."[9]

The attitude toward discipline in these Puritan congregations sprang from the same source. Discipline was a deeply serious and Spirit-centered response of the holy community toward its members. Its purpose was to maintain the purity and, therefore, the spiritual health of the body of Christ. There could be no health in the body if there was sickness in any of its members. If sickness were discerned, the gathered church as a whole was obliged to act in love to reprimand and thus cure a member, or, if necessary, to cast him or her out. Discipline that came out of the intimate, holy fellowship, the Puritans believed, was likely to be both more relevant and more just than discipline carried out by a remote ecclesiastical court.

The ideal of the gathered church and its tentative institutional expression took shape gradually. Its roots went back to Elizabethan times and the short-lived meetings known as "prophesyings." These were regional assemblies of clergy, designed to breathe new life into the church by training a preaching ministry to carry the good news of the gospel throughout the English countryside, following the dictum of the apostle Paul: "You can all prophesy one by one, so that all may learn and all be encouraged" (1 Cor. 14:31). For these Puritan leaders, to prophesy was to explain the Bible and interpret it in simple language so that people would understand just how the Christian message applied to them and how it could help them. Without prophecy, said Thomas Cartwright, a learned Elizabethan Puritan, the Bible is a "sealed book."[10]

In Northampton, the home of one of the most successful of the prophesyings, local clergy would gather on Saturday mornings from nine until eleven o'clock, at which time a young preacher would explain a prearranged biblical text to the assembled clergy and to the laity who had been invited to the exercise. This first speaker would be followed by four or five of his colleagues, expounding the same text in order of seniority. Later the laity would be dismissed and the clergy would share a meal, during which they discussed the merits of each other's preaching. In addition, these gatherings were often the focal point for the exercise of church discipline in the area.

Although, at their inception, the prophesyings were not intended to be subversive of the established church but only to give it new life, and although they were organized with the approval of Archbishop Grindal, they were nonetheless correctly perceived by the queen to be centers of potential unrest in her church and, therefore, in the nation. Queen Elizabeth I had never been much interested in either a preaching ministry or an educated laity. She preferred the safe simplicity of the sacraments preceded by a brief, prescribed homily. In 1577, she suppressed the prophesyings after a protracted struggle with her archbishop, their gallant defender. "Bear with me I beseech you, Madam," he had told his queen, "if I choose rather to offend your earthly majesty than to offend the heavenly majesty of God."[11] The archbishop was dismissed.

The prophesying movement could be suppressed, as were other reform movements after it, but the felt need that inspired it could not. The roots that had been planted began to spread underground. The reforming members of the clergy had become aware of one another, of who and where they were, and of the value of association for their own enrichment and for spreading the good news of the gospel.

Gradually, as a network in support of a preaching ministry grew, the ideal of the gathered church became increasingly articulated. And slowly, there began to appear—especially in East Anglia—little pockets of worshipers led by spiritual preachers who aspired to realize the ideal. By the 1620s two groups could be distinguished. The more radical group wanted immediate change: "reformation without tarrying for any," said Robert Browne, one of the most famous among them.[12] He and his sympathizers felt that in order to establish a true church they must separate completely from the Church of England. No true church could, they believed, be led and ministered to by outsiders such as a monarch or a bench of bishops, for whom the gathered church was both heresy and treason. These Congregationalists went into hiding where they formed small, exclusive church communities. To escape persecution many went to Holland, where some of them became the Pilgrims who founded Plymouth in New England.

A more moderate group of Congregationalists remained within the Church of England, its members called by Perry Miller, "non-separating congregationalists."[13] They believed that, although the Church of England as a whole was not a covenanted church, it could nonetheless, within its more rigorist congregations, *contain* a holy community and thus be considered a true church. Within a certain parish, for example, a group of parishioners who had been touched by the Spirit might gather together and either explicitly or implicitly covenant with one another. They would usually accept as their pastor the rector of their parish (if the rector were of their persuasion), an ordained lecturer who had been invited to serve them, or a local chaplain who served the household of a Puritan aristocrat. All of these varying arrangements were based in common on what was believed to be the essential core of the true church, a fellowship gathered in the Spirit. Sometimes the small churches-within-the-church were gathered formally, as in the case of John Cotton's in Boston, Lincolnshire; or they might be constituted informally, as in the case of Thomas Shepard's congregation in Earles Colne, Essex. Whatever the manner of their gathering, the clergy who served these congregations remained firmly within the Church of England. From this group of non-separating clergy came all of the leaders of the Massachusetts Bay Colony. We will trace their fortunes as they left their homeland and brought their vision of congeries of Reformed churches to New England, planting little gathered churches around the Shawmut Peninsula.

Planted in New England

As the Puritan movement spread and grew stronger, so too did the perception by its enemies that this religious revival was subversive to both church and state. The two developments fed into each other, and, as time went on, each gathered momentum. Under pressure, the Puritans became better organized and more radical in their disaffection from the established church. At the same time the monarchy and the church became increasingly suspicious of Puritan activities and more than ever determined to establish uniformity.

Before about 1628, however, enforcement of religious uniformity by the state was sporadic. Members of the Puritan clergy would be cited by the church courts or not, depending on how provocative their behavior was and on the varying attitudes of local bishops and their informants. Some were deprived of their pastorates and later reinstated. Some would conform briefly in order to remove themselves from serious scrutiny and then, when the danger was past, return to their Puritan ways. Others, like John Cotton of Boston in Lincolnshire, continued in relative freedom for long periods. Cotton managed to survive in his pastorate for twenty years, under three different bishops, in spite of his having established a covenanted community within his Church of England parish and consistently using a simplified form of worship.

In the 1630s, however, the uneasy balance of forces was disturbed for the Puritans, and they began to become seriously apprehensive about the future of their faith. The change in mood was brought about by forces both external to England and within the country. Puritan leaders watched with dismay the defeat of Protestant forces abroad at the opening of the Thirty Years' War and the capture of La Rochelle, the last Protestant bastion in Catholic France. At the same time, they watched and felt the effects of the rise of the High Church party under Charles I and, in particular, the king's increasing reliance on William Laud as Bishop of London and then, in 1633, as Archbishop of Canterbury.

Laud inspired intense emotions in his contemporaries. Puritans regarded him with dread and hatred. Thomas Shepard called him "a man fitted by God to be a scourge to his people."[14] His violent temper was acknowledged by his friends and feared by his foes. As one contemporary noted, "he had so little command of his passions that he could not repress them" even in the ecclesiastical courts.[15] And when he got angry, his normally ruddy complexion flushed brighter than ever. Remembering his own altercation with Laud, Shepard wrote that "he looked as though blood would have gushed out of his face."[16]

His admirers saw a different person in this severe and erect little man. In fact, as one of them expressed it, "so short of trunk never contained so much excellent treasure." They saw austerity of demeanor and enormous reserve in him. Above all they saw consistency. According to a careful observer,

> the blustering winds which so raged against him, did rather fix him at the root, than either shake his resolution, or force him to desist from his purpose in it. . . . He was always one and the same man: that beginning with him at Oxon, and so going on to Canterbury, he was unmoved and unchanged. . . he never complied with the times, but kept his own stand.[17]

This notable consistency in Laud was combined with a scrupulous integrity of purpose which sprang from his faith as well as from ambition. He was dedicated to the orderly reform of church and state in England with as much zeal and with as great and sustained a passion as his Puritan adversaries.

Laud's conception of a renewed, disciplined, and rededicated Church of England was, of course, very different from theirs. Rather than the spiritually new church with a simplified liturgy which inspired the Puritans, Laud was determined to revive the institutional strength of the old, pre-Reformation church in the firm belief that the Church of England could be made to serve the land with something like the completeness of the medieval church. He was determined to make his church again rich enough and strong enough to care for the poor; to provide for the education of its priests and to demand their devotion; to keep its buildings in repair; and, above all, to insist on uniformity of doctrine, liturgy, and ritual. Laud's commitment to absolute uniformity in the church was deep and lasted to the end. "Of all diseases," he said to the Long Parliament on the first day of the trial that followed his impeachment, "I have ever hated a palsy in religion, well knowing that too often a dead palsy ends that disease in the fearful forgetfulness of God and his judgments."[18]

In taking this position and advancing these goals Laud maintained that he was standing in line with national tradition, merely reasserting what the Church of England had long held. He insisted that he had made no innovations with respect to liturgy, his changes being but the "restoration of the ancient approved ceremonies, in, and from the beginning of the Reformation, and settled either by law or custom." He even spoke easily of "the Church of England and *other* [R]eformed churches."[19] His enemies felt that he belied such assertions with true innovations in both liturgy and doctrine.

Laud proceeded to realize his objectives for the church by initiating internal reforms and, more important for our purposes, by rigorously attacking external opposition, especially Puritan opposition. His attack took two forms. Dissident clergy were searched out and silenced far more thoroughly and systematically than before. Even more serious for the Puritan brethren were new developments in both liturgy and doctrine which they perceived to be potentially corrupting to their faith. When the laws of uniformity were enforced under Laud, it was with a new liturgical emphasis. The sacraments as vehicles of grace had become so important that it was feared they might override the great and irresistible grace of predestination.[20] A contemporary commented on the subtle change:

> When the ceremonies began to be urged upon the conscience with so much earnestness as if they had been necessary to salvation, men of tender conscience... began to fear, that they should transgress the commandments of God, by observing traditions... and conceived it vain to join with them in worship, who worshiped God in vain.[21]

Equally disturbing to Puritan leaders was their increasingly clear recognition that, theologically, Laud's ascendance marked a swing away from Reformed theology toward a less strictly predestinarian doctrine known as Arminianism, after Jacob Arminius of Holland.

From the late sixteenth century, Arminianism had presented the

Reformed consensus of the Church of England with a source of conflict, which was formally resolved in favor of the Reformed party at the Synod of Dort. The Synod was an assembly of the Dutch Reformed Church held in 1618–1619 and attended by international Reformed Church representatives who concurred with Dutch theologians in accepting its decrees. Unconditional election, the total depravity of humankind, and irresistible grace were declared to be the firm basis of Reformed theology and, therefore, of the theology of the Church of England.[22] An Arminian minority in England, however, continued to hold that there was indeed a measure of free will that could influence election. The penitent might, they believed, accept or reject grace when it was offered. James I, in spite of his Scottish heritage, supported them for largely political reasons. In 1620, only three years after the conclusion of the Synod, he issued a directive requiring that preachers below the rank of dean or bishop refrain from preaching "in any popular auditory the deep points of predestination, election, reprobation, or of the universality, efficacy, resistibility or irresistibility of God's grace"—all of the favorite doctrines of the Puritan clergy.[23] With such clear support from the king, the Arminian group quietly gathered influence. They surfaced openly in the favorable atmosphere created by the accession of Charles I and found a firm champion in his Archbishop of Canterbury. For the first time the Puritans began to feel a threat not only to their persons but to their very faith.

The deepening crisis produced a variety of responses among Puritans, responses that depended on individual personalities and circumstances. Some decided on conformity in the belief that the primary call was the pastoral one. A faithful shepherd, they believed, should tend his flock with an unswerving commitment, no matter what church authorities required. Expressing this view, the poet Francis Quarles asked what those sticklers for liturgical purity would say to God when they were called upon to account for the flocks they had deserted:

> O, what an answer will be given by some!
> We have been silenced; canons struck us dumb;

The Great ones would not let us feed thy flock
Unless we played the fool and wore a frock [surplice];

. . .

To say the truth, Great Judge, they were not fed;
Lord, here they be; but, Lord, they are all dead.'
Ah cruel shepherds! Could your conscience serve
Not to be fools and yet to let them starve?
What if your fiery spirits had been bound
To antick habits, or your heads been crowned
With peacocks plumes; had ye been forced to feed
Your Savior's dear bought flock in a fool's weed?
He that was scorned, reviled, endured the curse
Of a base death on your behalf; nay worse
Swallowed up the cup of wrath charged to the brim;
Durst ye not stoop to play the fools for Him?[24]

Other Puritan leaders may have conformed for reasons of ambition. It was said of Stephen Marshall, a famous preacher who rose high under Cromwell: "he was so supple a soul, that he brake not a joint, yea, sprained not a sinew in all the alteration of the times."[25] Still others took great personal risks by refusing to conform, enduring torture and imprisonment.

Another group decided on emigration, believing that the call to purity and singleness of heart in following God's word, as they understood it, came before all else. It was not an easy decision for them, as it was not for their colleagues who chose to remain in England and resist the authorities. Many of them had a great deal to lose. Hooker, Cotton, Nathaniel Ward, John Wilson, and Ezekiel Rogers, all of whom came to Massachusetts Bay in the 1630s, were in their forties and fifties with well established reputations and large families which had to be uprooted. Shepard, Roger Williams, John Eliot, and Samuel Stone were younger and had less to lose. They had all held insecure pastorates from the beginning, and all had been forced to move about frequently because of their persistent nonconformity. Their decision was less difficult, but difficult nonetheless. The most basic traumas of emigration were shared by young and old: sorrow at separation from home and family, fear of the perilous sea voyage and exile in the unknown wilderness beyond. Many immigrants also experienced a lingering sense of guilt about abandoning the Puritans who stayed behind in England, working and suffering for the faith they held in common. Shepard, as he considered departure, wondered whether "it was true I should stay and suffer for Christ" and care for those parishioners who "did desire me to stay in the north and preach privately."[26] Ultimately, the call to New England proved stronger. It provided an avenue for wholehearted commitment, an escape from chaos, and even a sense "that the act of renouncing England might have a cleansing effect on those who dared."[27] The decision to emigrate in the end provided for Shepard and the others relief, hope, and a rising sense of promise.

The attitude of the founders of New England toward the church they hoped to create in the New World grew out of their English experience. The zeal with which they approached the whole enterprise was the direct result of their encounter with the increasing tension and fear that had pervaded the gathered communities within the Church of England and had fanned the flames of spiritual commitment. Because of all they had endured and were enduring for their faith, they were determined to establish in New England a church and a society that would embody all they had fought for. They were exhilarated by the opportunity to establish the true church of Christ in virgin territory. The opportunity to fashion just what God wanted seemed unlimited.

They thought about these things even as they sailed to New England. John Winthrop's famous exhortation to the company aboard the flagship *Arbella* expresses the thrill of enthusiasm that filled his companions as well as the sober wisdom and generosity characteristic of him:

> *Whatsoever we did or ought to have done when we lived in England, the same must we do and more also where we go. That which the most in their churches maintain as a truth in profession only, we must bring into familiar and constant practice, as in*

this duty of love we must love brotherly without dissimulation, we must love one another with a pure heart fervently.... We must be willing to abridge ourselves of our superfluities, for the supply of others' necessities; we must uphold a familiar commerce together in all meekness, gentleness, patience and liberality. We must delight in each other, make others' conditions our own, rejoice together, mourn together, labor and suffer together, always having before our eyes our commission and community in the work, our community as members of the same body. So shall we keep the unity of the spirit in the bond of peace, the Lord will be our God and delight to dwell among us... for we must consider that we shall be as a city upon a hill, the eyes of all people are upon us. [28]

This remarkable lay sermon expresses well the depth of commitment and the power of the ideal that moved a whole people to New England.

Along with their zeal, these pilgrims brought with them a set of principles they would follow in organizing new churches, and guidelines that would shape the structure of their communities. Both principles and guidelines had, like their zeal, been forged out of their English experience.

The essentials of the new church were few and well formulated. A church would be gathered by a company of believers who were known to be upright and law-abiding people. They would confess their faith in Jesus Christ and join together in covenant, promising to walk in God's ways and to love and support one another. Finally, these covenanted Christians would elect a pastor from among themselves.

This gathered church was the spiritual body of Christ. Therefore, just as they had believed and practiced in England, no liturgy or ritual could be used that did not contribute to the building up of that body. In addition, as they had believed but had been unable to practice in England, discipline was to be exercised within the body to keep it pure and clean. A church founded upon these principles and upon these alone was held to be a true church.

Both John Cotton and Thomas Shepard, while they were in England, had maintained an unbroken allegiance to the Church of England, believing that it could and did contain within itself true, gathered churches. However, when they set sail for New England, they immediately disassociated themselves from the past and turned their faces to the pure churches they would found there. Both waited to have their baby sons baptized until they had established themselves in new, covenanted churches.

The polity of the new church was far more fluid in the minds of its founders than the principles upon which it was founded. They had, after all, no experience in founding a church in England. There had been no opportunity to try; and, in any case, the creation of a new church had not been their purpose. Their hope had been, instead, to give new life to the old Church of England, to convert its members to a lively faith, and to shelter and nurture small bands of the faithful gathered out of an indifferent or hostile community. Their role in New England was to be very different. There, as the sole architects of a new church—the only church in the land—they found themselves responsible for the spiritual life as well as the conduct of *all* the people, not merely the converted. The obligations acquired with this new responsibility, together with the general principles that they brought with them, gradually shaped the church that they built.

The clergy worked well together (although not without conflict) because they were of one fraternity, united by a common education and experience in England. They were used to consulting, praying, and making decisions together. John Wilson and John Cotton of Boston, Thomas Weld and John Eliot of Roxbury, Thomas Hooker and Samuel Stone of Cambridge and later of Hartford, Nathaniel Ward of Ipswich, Ezekiel Rogers of Rowley, and Thomas Shepard of Cambridge were all graduates of Cambridge University, and all at one time or another had been part of an East Anglian network of dissident clergy. In New England, by 1633, it was well established that "the ministers in the bay . . . [would] meet, once a fortnight, at one of their houses . . . where some question of moment was debated."[29]

The beginnings of the church that they built were tentative, flexible and, in some respects, democratic. However, within ten years, as a result of pressures both internal and external, the church structure had become clearly defined, much less democratic, and frequently both rigid and authoritarian.

The steps by which the earliest development of the Congregational Way was worked out are not entirely clear and have been the source of some scholarly controversy. According to a traditional story, when Dr. Samuel Fuller of Plymouth was called to the tiny new settlement of Salem in 1629 to give medical advice to the inhabitants, he was said to have advised them about more than their health, proceeding to instruct them in the procedures for gathering and maintaining a congregational church as it had been done in Plymouth. In the summer of 1630, he again visited Massachusetts Bay, this time with Edward Winslow, and offered more advice. Through these two encounters and other more informal contacts, the Plymouth church was said to have become the model for the churches subsequently founded in the Bay Colony.

Perry Miller challenged this long-accepted view by his reconstruction of the non-separating English communities which we have discussed above.[30] The leaders of these communities such as John Cotton, Thomas Hooker, and Thomas Shepard had had no practice in setting up congregational churches, but, as Miller pointed out, they would certainly have given careful thought to the procedures they would follow when given the opportunity.

Probably the truth lies somewhere in between the two points of view, or in a combination of the two. The leaders of Massachusetts Bay brought convictions and plans with them, but they clearly got much practical counsel from the Plymouth Colony.

From two early accounts we can learn a great deal about the first steps taken to establish a distinctive Congregational polity and about the earliest requirements for membership. The church in Salem was the first to be gathered in New England outside of Plymouth. A contemporary described the occasion:

> *They pitched upon the sixth of August for their entering into a solemn covenant with God, and one another, and also for the ordaining of their ministers; of which they gave notice to the*

church of Plymouth (that being the only church that was in the country before them) the people made choice of Mr. Skelton for their pastor and Mr. Higginson for their teacher. And accordingly it was desired of Mr. Higginson to draw up a confession of faith and covenant in Scripture-language; which being done was agreed upon. . . . Thirty copies of the foresaid confession of faith and covenant being written out for the use of thirty persons who were to begin the work. When the sixth of August came . . . after the sermons and prayers of the two ministers, in the end of the day, the foresaid confession of faith and covenant being solemnly read, the forenamed persons did solemnly profess their consent thereunto; and then proceeded to the ordaining of Mr. Skelton Pastor, and Mr. Higginson Teacher of the church there. Mr. Bradford the Governor of Plymouth and some others with him . . . gave the right hand of fellowship wishing all prosperity, and a blessed success unto such beginnings. [31]

Most of the essentials that we recognize as belonging to a gathered church are here: a voluntary gathering of the faithful who covenant together, who elect and ordain their leaders, and who are welcomed into a congregational fellowship by an already established church (a practice new in New England). What is noteworthy in this account in view of the subsequent evolution of a distinct "Congregational Way" in New England, is the manner in which the members were received. The founding thirty were required to "profess their consent" to a confession of faith that had been previously composed and of which each had a copy. Following their profession they covenanted together.

By the time that Thomas Shepard's church was gathered in New-town in February of 1636, the requirement for membership had changed. Here is John Winthrop's account of that day:

Mr. Shepard, a godly minister come lately out of England, and divers other good Christians, intending to raise a church body, came and acquainted their magistrates therewith, who gave their approbation. They also sent to all the neighboring churches for

> *their elders to give their assistance, at a certain day, at New-*
> *town, when they should constitute their body. Accordingly, at*
> *this day there met a great assembly, where the proceeding was as*
> *followeth: Mr. Shepard and two others (who were after to be*
> *chosen to office) sat together in the elder's seat. . . . Then the el-*
> *der desired to know of the churches assembled what number were*
> *needful to make a church, and how they ought to proceed in this*
> *action. Whereupon some of the ancient ministers, conferring*
> *shortly together, gave answer: that the Scripture did not set down*
> *any certain rule for the number. Three (they thought) were too*
> *few . . . but that seven might be a fit number. And, for their pro-*
> *ceeding, they advised, that such as were to join should make con-*
> *fession of their faith, and declare what work of grace the Lord*
> *hath wrought in them; which accordingly they did, Mr. Shepard*
> *first, then four others, then the elder, and one who was to be*
> *deacon, . . . and another member. Then the covenant was read,*
> *and they all gave a solemn assent to it. Then the elder desired of*
> *the churches, that, if they did approve them to be a church, they*
> *would give them the right hand of fellowship.* [32]

Here once again are the essential steps of gathering, covenanting, ordaining (in this case at a subsequent date), and reception by other churches. As the necessity of "conferring together" about the number of founding members shows, the manner of gathering was clearly still in a state of flux. New was the necessity of obtaining the permission of the General Court to found a church. Also new and by far the most important change to occur, was the dictum "that such as were to join" should not only "make confession of their faith" but also "declare what work of grace the Lord had wrought in them." Here was an entirely new requirement for church membership, a real departure from the process used in gathering any other churches either in Holland or in England. Before being accepted into the body of Christ, according to the new rule, one must have been touched by the Spirit and be able to testify to the experience. The concept was rooted in the teaching of the Apostle Paul, especially in 1 Cor. 12:13: "For in one Spirit we were all baptized into one body—Jews or Greeks, slaves or free—and we were all made to drink of one Spirit." That baptism by the Spirit became the key to church membership, and it was a requirement in sharp contrast to the assent to a creed or set confession necessary to admission to other churches, both Protestant and Roman Catholic.

Scholars do not know with any certainty why or how such an important change took place. A plausible guess is that the highly charged spiritual atmosphere in the early years of the planting of Boston was a contributing factor. We know that soon after his arrival in 1633 the charismatic preaching of John Cotton had an immediate and powerful effect on the already sensitive spiritual awareness in Boston. "It pleased the Lord," said John Winthrop, "to give special testimony of his presence in the church of Boston, after Mr. Cotton was called to office there. More were converted and added to that church, than to all the other churches in the bay."[33] Cotton's preaching emphasized the immanent presence of the Spirit and the wonder of unmerited grace. He spoke of the necessity of surrender "before the Lord in our spirits." It is this kind of faith, according to Cotton, that is the foundation of the covenanted church:

> if the church be built upon this rock; storms and winds not so much as shake it, it being built upon faith, and faith upon Jesus Christ: by this means the covenant will keep us constantly, sweetly, and fruitfully, in an everlasting kind of serviceable usefulness one to another.[34]

Given the yearning for direct contact with God, which had been a part of the Puritan consciousness from the beginning, and the extremity of the wilderness situation, it was perhaps natural that the preaching of John Cotton should produce an awareness of the Spirit which flowered into the most essential element of the gathered church in early New England. To form a virgin church made up only of believers who had been touched by the Spirit was to ensure its purity and its essential nature as a God-centered way of worship and living. It was to create a truly holy community.

In spite of many individual variations, the conversion narratives or "relations" of faith made by prospective church members belong to a distinct genre. To discover its philosophical and stylistic origin, we must return to England and look back again for a moment at a development in the predestinarian thinking of English Reformed theologians. In a subtle shift of emphasis, they began to move away from the high Calvinism of some of their colleagues, tending to become more concerned than their continental counterparts with the experiential aspect of their faith. As teachers and pastors, they began to explore the dynamics of conversion. They examined the experience of longing for encounter with the Spirit, of fear of rejection, and of grace if it should come. Their new interest in the process of conversion did not, however, mean that these theologians consciously turned away from the all-powerful God in whose hands human destiny rested. Rather, they continued to hold firmly that the human response to grace, although it might appear to come from the self, was ultimately the work of God.

This new direction received a systematic form in the latter half of the sixteenth century. Members of the Puritan clergy began to distinguish stages along the path that they believed a pilgrim traveled on the way to salvation. They described a pattern or order of salvation that they used to instruct eager and anxious Christians in how to approach the faith. Perhaps more important, the pattern served as well to comfort people by pointing out signposts that would indicate progress along the way to grace. It might even assure the penitent that, without clearly recognizing it, he or she had already experienced grace. Thus, although God was still in charge, humankind was given a sense through this kind of teaching, that at least cooperation was possible.

This *ordo salutis* or order of salvation worked out by the Puritan clergy evolved from an earlier history. It was rooted in the apostle Paul's description in Romans 8:28–30 of the manner in which "all things work together for good for those who love God, who are called according to his purpose." They are "predestined to be conformed to the image of his Son.... And those whom he predestined he also called; and those whom he called he also justified; and those whom he justified he also glorified." The progress of the believer from God's call or vocation to justification and to final glorification was explored by theologians and used by pastors throughout the Middle Ages. The Puritan formulation, however, was a kind of psychological elaboration of the concise scheme in Romans. With variations in emphasis, according to the background and temperament of different Puritan preachers in England and New England, the process began in a fashion somewhat as follows. An everyman or everywoman, in whom we would all recognize ourselves, is living a life of basic contentment with self—doing a little good and a little bad without thinking much about it. And then, one day, he or she is shaken from that easy complacency, usually by a sermon or a phrase from the Bible, perhaps even the word of a friend. A sudden intuition floods the penitent with the realization of sin. At that moment, or soon after, the sinner is aware of having broken God's law and being placed in mortal danger. This first, rational awareness was usually called "conviction" of sin. Conviction would be soon followed by an emotional awareness which would lead to a futile attempt by the sinner to change for the better by following the law. The attempt was doomed to failure because, even with the best will in the world, one cannot perfectly follow any law. The fruitlessness of even the most desperate effort would then convince the sinner of his or her powerlessness truly to change by any human exertion. At this point the confrontation with the law was most painful. It could produce prolonged inner turmoil, alternations between hope and fear, and perhaps even despair, which in itself was further evidence of sin. And so the sinner fell down, down, down.

Then, when all hope had been abandoned, came the approach of "humiliation." Humiliation meant the end of self-absorption and self-confidence and "release from the responsibilities of self-reliance."[35] It meant the freedom of turning to God with openness and in total submission. Then, and only then, could the Spirit move into the emptiness left by the self drained away, and take fast hold. The grace to believe that God loved the world with such infinite compassion as to send the Christ to die for humankind would come flooding in as the penitent was justified. The call would be personal and irresistible. "He hath made thee feel such an extreme need of him", said Thomas Shepard, "and made himself so exceeding sweet, that thou hast not been able to resist his love, but to cry out, Lord, thou hast overcome me with mercy, I am not able to resist any more."[36]

With the assurance of divine love, God's children would be transformed, restored from depravity to spiritual power and wholeness. They would see sin in a new light. No longer simply afraid of its consequences, they would come to mourn it because it separated them from God. Sin would, they saw, hurt and offend God, leaving them bereft. These grateful children would then be newly empowered by the presence of grace to change their way of life and to serve God with heart and soul and mind, a process they called "sanctification." The final step, called "glorification," united them with God after death.

When the process was complete, there remained a paradox as significant as any of the stages of the *ordo salutis*. A believer could never be sure of having been chosen. To be sure was, in fact, to be self-righteous, puffed up, lacking in humility, and, therefore, certainly not among the saints. Instead—and here is the paradox—continued intermittent periods of uncertainty and rigorous soul-searching were more probable signs of election. To be unsure of God's grace was perhaps to be saved.[37]

The first generation of New England preachers was educated in this tradition, and all had experienced conversions according to the accepted morphology, many after protracted and painful struggles. These were troubling as well as joyful experiences, which were deeply assimilated into their faith and used for the rest of their lives in counsel and exhortation. It is easy to understand in these circumstances that they would have chosen to make an experience of grace the qualification for membership in their gathered churches, since for them it was the pivotal point of their lives as Christians.

The question of the effect of such a requirement for membership on the communal feeling of the gathered churches is difficult to analyze at this removed date. At its worst, it probably fostered hypocrisy, self-righteousness, and exclusiveness as well as despair among those who in all honesty felt that they were unqualified. At its best, the test of faith enhanced both the spiritual vitality and the social usefulness of the New England churches, especially in the early years. To speak publicly of one's spiritual pilgrimage is an act demanding courage and spiritual intensity, and to hear others confess their faith is to relive one's own experience. It is to renew and enlarge one's own commitment. Public confession is also an intimate act. The speaker is exposed and vulnerable and, therefore, to be treated with tenderness and respect by the holy community. To join together in a covenant with God and in promise of support to one another after such a shared spiritual experience is to forge strong bonds of mutual support and care, bonds that were deeply needed by a people who were exiled across a wide ocean, many miles from home, and whose daily life in frontier communities was austere, hard, and unpredictable. The test for membership with all of its potential for self-righteousness, therefore, probably contributed to the stability of the gathered church and of the community. It was part of the foundation of church and commonwealth.

Building a church on this carefully laid foundation was not an orderly process. In the turmoil of theological and cultural changes over three hundred fifty years, the edifice has been frequently shaken. Its first shaking took place in Boston, even as its foundation was being laid.

Heresy in the Gathered Church

By the mid-1630s there were newly gathered churches scattered in a wide semicircle around the Shawmut Peninsula in Boston, Dorchester, Roxbury, Newtown, Watertown, Hingham, Dedham, and Concord. They were tightly bonded communities led by pastors and teachers who had come on a long journey with their followers and intended to shelter them and nurture them in New England as they had in their homeland. All, pastors and church members were knit together by covenant, and all were believers who could testify to an experience of grace.

The governance of the new churches lay—at least in theory and, to a large extent, in practice—in the hands of the individual congregations. At the moment of solemn covenant, the power to order all things within the church was embodied in the gathered membership. Theirs was the primary authority, and it included the power to admit and dismiss members, to exercise ecclesiastical discipline, and to elect pastor and teacher and the other church officers whose own power was derived from theirs. In the earliest years of the Bay Colony, these powers were exercised with varying degrees of ministerial guidance in an atmosphere of spiritual revival and some freedom of expression. This allowed congregational members to "prophesy" in church and to ask questions after the sermon or lecture. There was a lively sense among the Puritan clergy and their flocks that the ideal for which so much had been ventured had become a reality in well-disciplined, Spirit-centered churches; and they rejoiced in their achievement. They had built, said Thomas Shepard, "pure, chaste, virgin churches, not polluted with the mixture of men's inventions, nor defiled with the company of evil men."[38] When this precious new creation was threatened by heresy soon after it had begun to flourish, the clergy and magistrates of the Bay Colony reacted first with dismay and then with ferocity. Heresy meant dissension, and dissension they feared would place their whole enterprise in jeopardy, shaking the deepest values and the very stability of society.

It is difficult for us in the late twentieth century to imagine a commonwealth so greatly agitated by a matter of theology. But Massachusetts Bay society, unlike ours, was a society saturated with religion. There was among its citizens an acute sense of the hand of God in every occurrence, from great affairs of state to the minutiae of daily life. With death always near and life so unpredictable, one could depend only on God. In addition, every individual, to a greater or lesser degree, was of necessity preoccupied with the dynamics of faith. Churchgoers (and nearly everyone was a churchgoer) had either experienced a conversion according to the accepted order of salvation or, if they had not, were hoping to. They attended church for at least two hours, morning and afternoon on Sundays, as they had in England; and, in addition, many of them traveled to different towns to attend Thursday lectures. So great was the attendance at these Thursday meetings that daily work was being neglected and a law was passed curtailing them.

A conviction that the church and state must be closely allied, working in mutual support and cooperation, was an important consequence of the religious orientation of the holy commonwealth. To implement that cooperation, its laws were framed to be as close to the biblical model as possible. In addition, the franchise depended on church membership, as did election to the Great and General Court. Every important decision of state was made in consultation with the clergy. In such an atmosphere, it is not surprising that religious heresy profoundly shook Massachusetts when it appeared in the antinomian doctrines of a religious leader named Anne Hutchinson.

With this charismatic woman and the theological controversy that she provoked began a power struggle that penetrated every aspect of life in the Bay Colony. The basic issues lying beneath the struggle were obscured at the time by intense, nearly apocalyptic rhetoric on both sides. Today, although there remains a considerable scholarly controversy over the affair, it has become possible to sort out some of its dynamics and clearest components. An economic dimension is apparent in the remarkable predominance of merchants among Hutchinson's supporters, businesspeople who wanted to break the hold of Puritan laws restraining trade, such as the prohibition of usury and the adherence to price fixing according to the medieval teaching on the just price.[39] A vigorous political struggle for control erupted between Governor Winthrop and the young Sir Henry Vane, a Hutchinson convert recently arrived from England. A sexist dimension to the conflict appears in the emotional fury with which Hutchinson was attacked by magistrates and clergy in open revulsion against her unseemly behavior, her aggressiveness unbecoming a woman. Finally, on a purely human level, it was a conflict in which strong and colorful personalities were pitted against each other and which ended in great personal tragedy.

The adjective "antinomian" means "against-law" and was widely used in England and New England as a pejorative term to describe those who considered themselves to be set free from the moral law by virtue of being in a state of grace. These seekers after God were said to believe that they had been so transformed by the touch of the Spirit that they knew with perfect clarity God's will for them. They no longer felt any need of the law, even as a prescriptive guide for conduct, because they knew in their very souls what God wanted and could, therefore, spontaneously do God's will.

An antinomian potential was latent in Christianity from its inception. The apostle Paul vigorously denounced critics who "slander us" with the accusation of taking the Mosaic Law lightly (Rom. 3:8). The Gnostic heresy of the second century had an antinomian component; and, in the sixteenth century, the tendency resurfaced on the continent in the preaching of Anabaptists.

If we look for the wellspring of antinomianism in seventeenth-century England, it can be found in the nature of Puritanism itself. There was a strain of antinomianism among Puritans from the beginning. Puritanism, in fact, tended to produce antinomians on its fringes and then turn on them in fury and fear. The emphasis in Puritan spirituality on conversion, on waiting expectantly for the Spirit and on the holy community gathered in the Spirit, tended to produce believers among the most sensitive converts who felt themselves to have been infused by the Spirit and transformed into new beings. They had become vehicles of grace and could even speak God's will out of their direct encounter with the Spirit.

Although New England provided a fertile ground for the growth of antinomian ideas, the heritage of Puritan radicalism came from England, where religious communities with antinomian leanings began to appear in the seventeenth century, especially in the West Riding of Yorkshire. There were Grindletonians, so-called because they were centered in the town of Grindleton, where they had been inspired by their charismatic preacher, Roger Brierly. Brierly would gather crowds from his own and surrounding towns to hear him preach in the meadows outside of Grindleton. He preached what was actually a rather orthodox message of repentance and salvation. But his was Spirit-centered preaching, which emphasized the transformation of the soul after conversion. There were also Seekers, Ranters, and Quakers. Pendle Hill—where a vision came upon George Fox, founder of the Quakers—is close to Grindleton. And there was the Family of Love, a group founded by the Dutch mystic Hendrik Niclaes, who preached eloquently about the union of the converted soul with the Spirit. His message spread from Holland to England, and "familist," like "antino-mian," became an insulting epithet, suggesting moral laxity, in both England and New England.

To recount the story of Anne Hutchinson and the turmoil into which her antinomian inspiration cast the Bay Colony, we must begin in England, in the hamlet of Alford in Lincolnshire, twenty miles from the coastal town of Boston. There in 1591 she was born Anne Marbury, the daughter of Francis Marbury who, although he later con-formed, was in his youth a rebellious and vociferous clergyman who had been in prison three times before he was twenty-three as a result of his spirited preaching. Like so many women of distinction in the past, Anne Hutchinson received from her father the attention and tutelage which in her time were ordinarily reserved for a son. But Marbury had no son, at least not when his daughter was very young, and he had plenty of free time, having been deprived of his living shortly before her birth. So he taught her what he knew and what he believed. He also seems to have taught her to be independent and rebellious like himself. From her mother she learned the "womanly arts" which would focus her adult life: the administrative skills required to manage a large household of children, servants, and apprentices; the art of nursing the sick; and the expertise necessary to concoct compounds of herbal medicines and ointments. Just after her twenty-first birthday in 1612, she was married to William Hutchinson, a well-to-do sheep farmer from Alford and settled with him in a large house there. In less than a year the first of their fifteen children was born and Anne Hutchinson began the career of mothering, managing, nursing, and midwifery which occupied the rest of her life.

At about the time of their marriage, the Hutchinsons began to at-tend church in Boston, where John Cotton, the distinguished Puritan preacher from Emmanuel College in Cambridge, had recently been called. It was an unusual parish in that the church living was con-trolled by the town corporation; thus a call from Boston was very nearly a genuine congregational call at a time when, of course, most church appointments were episcopal appointments. While he was there, Cotton, as we have seen, carried his congregation even further toward congregationalism by establishing a covenanted community within the church.

That John Cotton was able to maintain his pastorate from 1613 until 1632, unmolested by church authorities, was considered a marvel by his colleagues. "Of all men in the world'" said Samuel Ward, a neighboring Puritan pastor, "I envy Mr. Cotton of Boston most; for he doth nothing in way of conformity, and yet hath his liberty and I do everything that way, and cannot enjoy mine."[40] Cotton's survival was due in part to his amiable personality and in part to the aldermen of Boston, who dealt expertly with the political repercussions of his behavior. His scholarly, kindly, and rather unworldly ways propelled him deeply into controversy in Boston, Massachusetts, where he had no one to advise him in political reality. In Lincolnshire, however, he was kept safe until 1632.

The Hutchinsons regularly traveled the twenty miles from Alford to hear Cotton preach during those years. Anne Hutchinson, in particular, found his preaching and his counsel a strength and inspiration. When in 1632 he was called before the Court of High Commission and then fled to New England with Thomas Hooker and Samuel Stone, she found his loss hard to bear. "When our teacher came to New-England it was a great trouble unto me," she testified at her trial, "and I could not be at rest but I must come hither."[41]

When John Cotton arrived in New England to share the Boston pulpit as teacher with John Wilson, the pastor, he was fifty years old, renowned as a preacher, and sure of his power. As we have seen, he was immediately successful in his new parish as the mainspring of a revival that swept the town during his first year there, doubling the size of the congregation. Cotton's was an orthodox Calvinist message. He did not preach to prepare the heart for salvation through the morphology of conversion, as most New England preachers did. Instead, he insisted on the radical impotence of men and women to influence the approach of the Spirit and on the impossibility of changing one's life without the grace of God. "I confess," Cotton asserted, "I do not discern that the Lord worketh and giveth any saving preparations in the heart till he give union with Christ." Grace, when it came, was overwhelming and irresistible. "If the Lord mean to save you, he will rend, as it were, the caul from the heart," he preached.[42] And then followed the blinding wonder of unmerited saving grace that left the believer permanently changed and in intimate relation with the Spirit. As "a wind-mill hath its motion, not only from the water, but in the water; so a Christian lives, as having his life from Christ, and in Christ," he wrote.[43]

Anne Hutchinson well knew Cotton's message, and when she arrived in Boston with her family she rejoiced to be once more part of his flock. She was forty-three in 1634, the mother of eleven surviving children. She and William quickly established themselves in church and community. William became a prosperous merchant, deputy to the General Court, and deacon of the church, "a very honest and peaceable man of good estate," said John Winthrop.[44] He was also, Winthrop observed elsewhere, one of "weak parts and wholly guided by his wife." Anne, on the other hand, impressed the Governor as "a woman of ready wit and bold spirit."[45] She continued in Boston to use her enormous vitality and generous spirit in the service of her neighbors, as she had in Alford. She nursed the sick, counseled the lonely, and offered her skills as midwife.

She also held meetings in her home to discuss the powerful sermons of John Cotton, and this was how her troubles began. The practice of holding small meetings to nurture and spread the faith had been common in England in the heat of persecution and even earlier. It was natural that this practice should continue in the revival atmosphere of Boston. At first, the meetings were not only legal but encouraged. However, under the leadership of Hutchinson, they began to arouse the apprehension of the magistrates and clergy. Filled with the excitement of Cotton's message, she was eager to express it to others. Cotton was at first gratified, and encouraged her participation in the spiritual revival that was taking place. However, as the weeks went on, it gradually became clear, at least to some observers, especially to John Wilson and to some clergy outside of Boston, that Mrs. Hutchinson had added a new dimension to her teacher's faith. Cotton's extreme emphasis on the freeness of grace, his deep and complete separation of grace and behavior or works, and his emphasis on the ecstasy of union with Christ, created an ethos that for a woman of Anne Hutchinson's gifts and temperament was intoxicating. She began to sense in herself, and to preach in her meetings, a state of grace beyond the law, in which one might dwell in the Spirit in conscious union with God.

If her message had gone no further, had remained simply one of mystical union with God, and had she continued to live with the generosity that was always her way, she very likely would have been left alone. As time went on, however, she became more and more obsessed with the dichotomy between grace and works. At the same time as her influence increased, so too did her self-confidence, her aggressiveness, and her conviction of the absolute truth of her position.

Filled with inspiration and secure in her understanding of doctrine, Anne Hutchinson pointed a finger of scorn at those members of the clergy (and their followers) whom she considered preachers of a covenant of works rather than the covenant of grace proclaimed by John Cotton. The result was the rapid growth of an alarming division within the churches, especially within the church in Boston. The accusation of preaching a covenant of works was a particularly stinging insult to the Puritan clergy, who as builders of holy communities gathered in the Spirit considered themselves to be bearers of the good news of the covenant of grace. They may also have felt a twinge of recognition, as Mrs. Hutchinson castigated them for a rigidity reminiscent of the Laudian legalism from which they had so recently fled. In particular, she spoke vehemently against a tendency of some among the clergy to assert, by way of comfort to their flocks, that a habit of consistent moral behavior was very probably evidence of the presence of the Holy Spirit in the life of a convert, an assertion that she believed was bound to lead would-be believers to the false assumption that good works would be rewarded by grace.[46] The followers of Anne Hutchinson, on the other hand, preached a union with Christ that was unrelated to any evidence of godly behavior. "I seek not for sanctification, but for Christ," they cried. "Tell me not of meditation and duties, but tell me of Christ."[47]

John Wilson was singled out for particular criticism. He was a rather stiff and proper person, ill-equipped to ride with the storm. First anguish and then quiet fury gripped him as Hutchinson and her followers interrupted his sermons with questions and insulted him by "contemptuously turning their backs upon the faithful pastor... and going forth from the assembly when he began to pray or preach."[48]

The lines between the factions soon became clearly drawn. The Hutchinsonian party was strengthened by the addition of two distinguished newcomers. In the fall of 1635, Henry Vane, the attractive and lively young son of Sir Henry Vane, Privy Councilor to Charles I, arrived from England and was immediately drawn into the meetings at the Hutchinsons' and captivated by the message that he heard there. Boston was also captivated by him and elected him Governor in the spring. That same spring the Reverend John Wheelwright, brother-in-law of Anne Hutchinson and a popular preacher in the vein of John Cotton, arrived in Boston. With the addition of these two men of influence to the Boston church, enthusiasm for the Hutchinsonian position grew until it swept nearly the whole church, excepting only the pastor and John Winthrop. Outside of Boston the clergy remained orthodox and highly critical of the goings-on there. Many of them, like John Wilson, had been derided as preachers of a covenant of works. Most vehement among the critics were Thomas Shepard of Newtown, Peter Bulkley of Concord, and Thomas Weld of Roxbury. John Winthrop described the mounting tension:

> Every occasion increased the contention and caused great alienation of minds; and the members of Boston (frequenting the lectures of other ministers) did make much disturbance by public questions, and objections to their doctrines, which did anyway disagree from their opinions; and it began to be as common here to distinguish between men, by being under a covenant of grace or a covenant of works, as in other countries between Protestants and Papists.[49]

A succession of decisive events between October 1636 and March 1638 escalated the tension and seemed to make inevitable the progress toward the trial, banishment, and excommunication of Anne Hutchinson.

October 1636: The Hutchinson group attempted to install John Wheelwright in the Boston pulpit to serve as a second teacher with Cotton and, of course, with John Wilson as pastor. The attempt was successfully blocked by John Winthrop.

December 1636: At a meeting of the General Court, John Wilson openly laid blame for the rising unrest on Governor Vane and on Anne Hutchinson. At the end of the session, a fastday of repentance and prayer for the restoration of order was called for January 20.

January 20, 1637: In his fastday sermon, John Wheelwright, who had been invited to be a guest preacher in Boston, delivered a sermon in which he "inveighed against all that walked in a covenant of works . . . and stirred up the people against them with much bitterness and vehemency," as Winthrop later reported.[50] The fastday, which had been intended to restore peace, had further deepened the controversy.

March 9, 1637: A meeting of the General Court addressed the unrest. Wheelwright was tried and condemned for sedition and contempt, in spite of a petition in his support being presented by the Boston Church. Sentencing was postponed until the next session because of the charged, pro-Hutchinsonian atmosphere in Boston. It was voted "with much heat of contention," said Winthrop, to hold that session, a court of election, at Newtown.[51]

May 17, 1637: Thomas Shepard preached the Election Day sermon on the Newtown Common preceding a chaotic election in which Vane was defeated and Winthrop chosen Governor. Once again, the sentencing of Wheelwright was put off, and once again Winthrop described the scene: "There was great danger of a tumult that day; for those of [Mrs. Hutchinson's] side grew into fierce speeches, and some laid hands on others."[52]

August 30, 1637: A synod of church leaders from all over New England was held at Newtown in the meeting house. Thomas Hooker came from Hartford and, with Peter Bulkley of Concord, moderated the meeting, which after twenty-five days identified a theological "Catalogue" of eighty-two "Erroneous Opinions," each followed by a "Confutation."

Four examples will indicate why orthodox and law-abiding magistrates and members of the clergy feared for their commonwealth and their church. Error 4, "That those that be in Christ are not under the Law and commands of the word, as the rule of life," could lead to social anarchy if implemented. Error 54, "No minister can be an instrument to convey more of Christ unto another, than he by his own experience hath come unto," was anti-intellectual and anticlerical in the extreme. Error 56, "Man is not effectually converted till he hath full assurance," left no room for the doubting, timid believer. Error 71, "The immediate revelation of my good estate, without any respect to the Scriptures, is as clear to me, as the voice of God from Heaven to Paul," opened the way for new revelation, direct from God.[53]

November 2, 1637: The General Court, now confidently controlled by the anti-Hutchinsonians, proceeded to pass sentence on Wheelwright. He and some of the members of the Boston church who had signed the petition in his favor were disenfranchised and banished.

November 15, 1637: The trial of Anne Hutchinson began before the General Court in the meetinghouse in Newtown, where it had been moved because of the overwhelming presence of Hutchinsonian partisans in Boston.

The tragedy and the high drama of the trial have been preserved for us to relive and ponder. One version was recorded by John Winthrop, the other by an unknown reporter. The latter, which will be quoted here, is an unadorned recording of the proceedings that vividly brings to life the verbal sparring and the intense emotion that filled the court sessions.[54]

In the austere and cramped space of the little frame meetinghouse on the corner of present-day Dunster and Mount Auburn Streets were brought together some of the most vigorous and colorful personalities in the Bay Colony. Present to confront Mrs. Hutchinson were Governor Winthrop and Deputy Governor Thomas Dudley as well as the assistants and deputies of the Great and General Court. Sitting with them were ministers from Salem, Boston, Roxbury, Watertown, and Cambridge. Most of these people were Mrs. Hutchinson's adversaries. John Cotton and Deputies John Cogshall, William Colburn, and William Coddington of Boston alone supported her. Most of the participants knew one another well, some as friends and associates from English days. Others had formed new friendships or animosities from the forced intimacy of small-town, frontier living. John Winthrop and Anne Hutchinson, the two central figures in the proceedings, instinctively had rubbed each other the wrong way from the beginning, and the daily unavoidable contact of neighbors living across the street from one another had increased their mutual dislike.

The assembly was a literate gathering, ranging from a learned clergy to magistrates who, if not widely read, were all thoroughly familiar with the Bible. Anne Hutchinson, although lacking in formal education, showed herself to be a formidable and at times dazzling opponent, even for the clergy: a woman, "of nimble wit and active spirit and a very voluble tongue, more bold than any man," John Winthrop admitted with some bitterness.[55] With a particular knowledge of the Bible at her fingertips and a verbal virtuosity far surpassing that of most laity, she confounded her adversaries at every turn, until finally, in an ingenuous and candid admission of her antinomian persuasion, she brought herself down.

The trial opened in an atmosphere of tension, a tension further increased by the informality of the proceedings which gave full range to the emotions of the participants. This was not a courtroom constrained by awe of the judiciary and the majesty of the law. It was, instead, a scene in which hostile and frequently inconclusive wrangling was interrupted from time to time by frustrated but determined attempts by the prosecutors to focus the trial and get on with the business of restoring order to their society.

The trial began with a statement by the governor, setting forth its purpose as he saw it:

Mrs. Hutchinson, you are called here as one of those that have troubled the peace of the commonwealth and the churches here . . . therefore we have thought good to send for you to under- stand how things are, that if you be in an erroneous way we may reduce you that so you may become a profitable member here among us, otherwise if you be obstinate in your course that then the court may take such course that you may trouble us no fur- ther. (312)

Immediately the wrangling began, in part because of the lack of specificity of the Puritan laws grounded in the Ten Commandments. "What law have I broken?" asked Mrs. Hutchinson. "Why, the fifth commandment," was the reply of the governor (313). Mrs. Hutchin- son had, in fact, broken no written laws of the Commonwealth. The Decalogue could be invoked, however, and made specific where it was deemed applicable by the magistrates in consultation with the clergy of the Bay Colony. In supporting John Wheelwright, in continuing to conduct meetings in her house that had been forbidden by the Gen- eral Court some months earlier, and in disparaging the majority of the clergy, Anne Hutchinson was accused of disobedience to "the fathers of the commonwealth"; this was the charge that had to be proven.

Unable to extract an admission of disobedience from Mrs. Hutchin- son in the matter of her support of John Wheelwright and his adher- ents, whom she said she "put honor upon . . . as the children of God and as they do honor the Lord," Winthrop in exasperation concluded this part of the testimony with the words: "We do not mean to dis- course with those of your sex but only this: you . . . do endeavor to set forward this faction and so you do dishonor us" (314).

Then Winthrop moved on to a second accusation, charging Mrs. Hutchinson with having, as a woman, illegally held household meet- ings. These she justified immediately with a biblical reference: "there lies a clear rule in Titus, that the elder women should instruct the younger" (Titus 2:3–5). Confounded here, Winthrop accused her of teaching men as well, provoking the rejoinder, "Do you think it not lawful for me to teach . . . and why do you call me to teach the court?"

"We do not call you to teach the court but to lay open yourself," was Winthrop's rejoinder (315).

With the testimony again inconclusive, the tactics were changed once more, this time by Deputy Governor Dudley. He steered the accusation away from the unseemliness of Hutchinson's meetings to their subversiveness. "Mrs. Hutchinson," he said, "hath so forestalled the minds of many by their resort to her meeting that now she hath a potent party in the country," and, "she in particular hath disparaged all our ministers in the land that they have preached a covenant of works, and only Mr. Cotton a covenant of grace" (318).

A long testimony followed. The ministers and some of the deputies made charges, and Mrs. Hutchinson made rebuttals with the support of Colburn and Coddington and, until near the end of the trial, John Cotton. As the day wore on, all parties became weary and hungry. Then, of her own volition, unaware of the effect that her words would have on the court, Anne Hutchinson candidly explained the source of her attitude about the clergy. She told how, as once she meditated on a passage from Scripture (Heb. 9:16), the Lord

> did give me to see that those which did not teach the new covenant had the spirit of antichrist, and upon this did discover the ministry unto me and ever since. I bless the Lord he did let me see which was the clear ministry and which the wrong (336).

Asked by one of the deputies, "How do you know that that was the spirit?" her reply was, "By an immediate revelation." "How!" cried the deputy governor, "an immediate revelation." Answered Mrs. Hutchinson, "By the voice of his own spirit to my soul. . . . Ever since that time I have been confident of what he hath revealed to me" (337).

The reaction was immediate. Here were all the fears of the leaders ingenuously and simply laid before them.[56] The specter of chaos was in their midst. "These disturbances that have come among the Germans have all been grounded upon revelations," said the deputy governor, "and so they that have vented them have stirred up their hearers to take up arms against their prince and to cut the throats one of another" (343). "This runs to enthusiasm," said the Reverend Hugh Peter. "It overthrows all," said the governor, adding, "I am persuaded that the revelation she brings forth is a delusion." And then: "All the court but some two or three ministers cry out, we all believe it—we all believe it" (343).

The hearing hastened to a conclusion. The governor held a vote:

> *The court hath . . . declared themselves satisfied . . . concerning the troublesomeness of her spirit and the danger of her course amongst us, which is not to be suffered. Therefore if it be the mind of the court that Mrs. Hutchinson for these things . . . is unfit for our society, and if it be the mind of the court that she shall be banished out of our liberties and imprisoned till she be sent away, let them hold up their hands.* (347)

Only two deputies, William Coddington and William Coburn, voted nay to the sentence of banishment. Still confident of the presence of the Spirit, Mrs. Hutchinson asked, "I desire to know wherefore I am banished." "Say no more," was Winthrop's rejoinder, "the court knows wherefore and is satisfied" (348).

Banishment was not yet to take place, however. In this commonwealth where church and state were so closely allied, the sentence of banishment could not be carried out until after the completion of a trial for heresy before the Boston church. Throughout the winter of 1637–1638 Hutchinson was confined in the home of Joseph Weld of Roxbury, brother of Thomas Weld, the pastor there. It was a painful and debilitating winter for her. At forty-six, and having borne fifteen children, she was pregnant once again. Ill and depressed but still filled with her private sense of the Spirit, she spoke of her faith with those members of her family who were allowed to visit her and with some members of the clergy who came to reason with her. To Thomas Shepard and Thomas Weld, in particular, she expressed herself eagerly and openly.

A church trial was held on the Lecture Day, March 15, 1638, in the Boston meetinghouse.[57] Mrs. Hutchinson arrived late, as one of the elders reported to the congregation, "not out of any contempt or neglect . . . but because she hath been long [under] durance. She is so weak that she conceives herself not fit nor able to have been here so long together" (351). Formal proceedings began immediately with "members of the congregation" requested to "draw as near together as they can . . . that when their consent or dissent is required . . . we may know how they do express themselves" (351). The ministers who tried Anne Hutchinson were deeply convinced of the rightness, even holiness, of their cause. They hoped by their proceedings to bring her to repentance and reunion with the church. "I know [not]," said Shepard, "wherein I could deal more lovingly with this your sister than to bring her thus before you." (353)

A list of errors compiled by Weld and Shepard from their interviews with Anne Hutchinson during her imprisonment was read as the substance of the charges. In response to her accusation that the two had come, with an intent unknown to her, "to entrap" her by their seemingly solicitous questions, they asserted, first, that she was "a very dangerous woman to sow her corrupt opinions to the infection of many" and, second, that both Weld and Shepard had come "to deal with her and labor to reduce her from her errors" privately before accusing her in public (353–54).

With her usual clarity of mind, she questioned her accusers as to precisely what they meant by their charges of doctrinal error. Some of the accusations had come up in the proceedings at Newtown or had been enumerated in the earlier list of "erroneous opinions." A new charge, dealt with at length, was that she had denied the immortality of the soul and the resurrection of body and soul "at the last day," emphasizing instead "our union to Christ Jesus" (351). Cotton was horrified and spoke harshly of the danger to society inherent in the belief that we "neither fear Hell nor the loss of Heaven." "What need we care what we speak," he continued, "or do, here if our souls perish and die like beasts" (372). The sanctions encouraging godly behavior would be wiped away by such doctrine.[58] Hutchinson insisted that these had not formerly been her beliefs, maintaining that, "I did not hold any of these things before my imprisonment" (372). And for a time after this she seemed penitent. In the end, battered by increasingly hostile questioning as she continued to search for clarity, she stated that her error had been not so much in doctrine as in expressing herself: "I confess my expression was that way but it was never my judgment" (378). These were not the words of true repentance according to her accusers. John Cotton, her long-revered and greatly beloved teacher, summed up the sense of the meeting:

> Though she have confessed that she sees many of the things which she held to be errors and that it proceeded from the root pride of spirit, yet I see this pride of heart is not healed but is working still, and therefore to keep secret some unsound opinions. God hath let her fall into a manifest lie, yea to make a lie and therefore as we received her amongst us I think we are bound upon this ground to remove her from us and not to retain her any longer, seeing she doth prevaricate in her words, as that her judgment is one thing and her expression is another. (385)

The excommunication was pronounced by John Wilson:

> In the name of our Lord Jesus and in the name of the Church . . . I do cast you out. . . . I do deliver you up to Satan. . . . I command you . . . as a leper to withdraw yourself out of the congregation. (388)

The air of tension and tragedy conveyed by the reports of the two trials of Anne Hutchinson is nearly overwhelming, and it is made even more acute by the frequent failure of both sides to communicate in language that was mutually understood. The adversaries reviled one another and yet each was unheard by the other, increasing their frustration and deepening the gap between them. It was a situation arising from both personality and circumstance. Although Hutchinson's knowledge of the Bible was remarkable and her mind sharp and quick, her education had been undisciplined and highly individual. Her use

of words seemed imprecise and even deceitful to her adversaries because of her sense that words are indeed imperfect representations of
reality and that expressions of religious truth must always be fragmentary. Such an attitude was infuriating and incomprehensible to the
Cambridge Masters of Arts, schooled in logic, who opposed her. Her
insistence on the importance of the personal context in which she had
spoken, whether it was "in a way of friendship privately," or "before a
public magistracy," seemed devious and irrelevant to her would-be
judges (319). Over and over again, Hutchinson appeared to her accusers to be intractable and to have "made a lie," at least in part because
of the cultural, educational, and gender gap that lay between them. It
was a gap that hastened and intensified her eventual condemnation.[59]

Excommunicated and banished, Anne Hutchinson moved first to
Rhode Island to join her family and fellow exiles. Then, after the
death of William in 1643, she moved to Pelham Bay on Long Island
with six of her children and their families. There, she and all of her
family except ten-year-old Susanna were killed in an Indian raid.
"Thus the Lord heard our groans to heaven," wrote Thomas Weld,
"and freed us from this great and sore affliction."[60]

Order was once more restored in the Bay Colony. At the same
time, in the conservative reaction that issued from the conflict,
the social and religious fabric of the Commonwealth was radically
changed. The hierarchical authority upon which the society was built
and which had been threatened by Hutchinson as a woman and as a
dissident, was reaffirmed. The Hutchinsonians were disarmed and
banished. Political stability and social homogeneity were reinforced in
May of 1637 when the court, in the heat of the controversy, ordered
that no new immigrants would henceforth be allowed to settle in the
jurisdiction of the Bay Colony without the approval of the magistrates. In addition, to prevent circumvention of the directive, a pen-
alty was to be imposed on all who even entertained a visitor for more
than three weeks. The purpose was made specific by Winthrop: he and
the other magistrates feared that the Hutchinsonians "expected many
of their opinion to come out of England."[61]

Of potential seriousness for the vitality of the churches was the curtailment of congregational power and freedom of expression. The considerable responsibility of the congregation for church governance and the spontaneity of congregational self-expression that had been encouraged by the clergy in the revival atmosphere of the earliest years had swung out of their control in the Antinomian Controversy and left them in a fearful and repressive frame of mind. The atmosphere in the 1640s was no longer one of revival. Instead, it was a time of longing for order, and this resulted in increased formalism. Congregational power was tempered with ministerial authority and spontaneity with repression. In 1637, at the height of the controversy, the freedoms to prophesy and to question the minister in church were abolished. By the end of the decade, congregational ordination was rare, having been replaced with ordination by ruling elders or other ministers. Church admission and dismissal as well as discipline were increasingly handled privately by the clergy before a formal presentation to the congregation was made. A ministerial veto over any majority congregational vote was introduced into the Cambridge Platform of 1648 to complete clerical control. Many of these changes were embodied in the Cambridge Platform, which for the first time formally set forth the "Congregational Way." Others were asserted in practice, although not necessarily on paper.[62]

Theologically, the Antinomian Controversy produced a clearer definition of New England Congregational orthodoxy. The particular blending of continental and English Reformed Church tenets that had held sway in the early years of the Bay Colony was modified in reaction to the radical doctrine and behavior of the antinomians. This radicalism that, as we have seen, was an ingredient in Puritan spirituality from the beginning, was suppressed and all but disappeared in the years following the crisis. At the same time, the doctrines that the antinomians had so ardently opposed became more securely rooted than ever. The importance of preparatory steps as a guide leading to conversion was reaffirmed and—more crucial to an even more basic issue of the Antinomian Controversy—the nature of the conversion process itself was clarified. Gone was the passive convert overwhelmed by the Spirit who gave assurance of salvation to the believer "by immediate light," as Cotton had said. In place of this convert was one more cautious, one who might come to conversion little by little, who might be given the grace to cooperate with God in finding the faith that brings justification, and who might find assurance in the acts of a godly life and in the very fact of believing.[63] This somewhat more rational, perhaps more legalistic theology became the predominant one in New England, at least into the time of Jonathan Edwards, one hundred years later.

Persisting through all the tumult, and in spite of the new legalism, was the ideal of the church that had been gathered in the Spirit. There remained at its core the warm spirituality that had so characterized Puritans from the beginning and that made the emphasis on conversion of continuing importance. The Cambridge Platform affirmed, for all to know and hear, that "A Congregational church" is one that consists "of a company of saints by calling, united into one body, by a holy covenant, for the public worship of God, and the mutual edification of one another, in the fellowship of the Lord Jesus." A concrete expression of widespread admission practice was also embedded in the platform in order to ensure that the membership truly did consist of "saints by calling." Henceforth, except in cases of "excessive fear or other infirmity," members were to be admitted after making "a personal and public confession and declaring of God's manner of working upon the soul."[64] The requirement was not uninfluenced by the conservative swing of the times, however. Originally designed to ensure the Spirit-centeredness of the gathered church, it probably became a tool increasingly used to sift out the unorthodox as prospective members.[65] A newly defined and newly shaped "Congregational Way" thus became the firmly established way, and its leaders were able—at least for a time—to teach its doctrine and carry out its discipline without opposition.

The early creativity of the New England churches, the tumult of the Antinomian Controversy, and the conservative reaction that followed it, are clear themes in the early history of the first church in Cambridge. But before turning to that discussion, we will examine the English ministry of Thomas Hooker and Thomas Shepard to provide background for the story of their church.

2

"PHYSICIANS OF THE SOUL"

Introduction

The Puritan divines of the sixteenth and seventeenth centuries in England were evangelists of a special kind. They called themselves "physicians of the soul."[1] As physicians, they not only called out sinners to turn to God and to learn to walk in his ways as did other evangelists, but they also carefully analyzed the anatomy of the soul. Then, if it was found to be ailing, they prescribed for it techniques of self-examination and programs of spiritual therapy that would heal it and bring it to wholeness in God. The pastor, Hooker said, "is the physician that God hath appointed whereby all the sickness of the soul may be eased and cured."[2]

This approach was part of the ministry of all Puritan preachers, but Hooker was a specialist in the process. One scholar has said of the body of his sermons that it contains: "the most minute and searching analysis of the soul and the process of spiritual regeneration, the most coherent and sustained expression of the essential religious experience ever achieved by the New England divines."[3] Thomas Shepard was Hooker's protégé and was deeply influenced by him. His objectives were like Hooker's, but his conception of the kind of care that heals proved to be significantly different.

Thomas Hooker: Leicestershire, Cambridge, Essex

Thomas Hooker was born on July 7, 1586, two years before the Spanish Armada. It was a heady time of emerging national consciousness in England. The country was fast becoming a great power filled with a new sense of military glory and patriotism and enjoying a literary renaissance. It was a time of some turbulence, too, of physical and emotional violence and deep sensibility that found expression in the high drama of Shakespeare and Marlowe and in the tenets of Calvinism. Increased commercial activity brought social mobility and the unrest that inevitably goes with it. There was also unrest, as we have seen, within the church. The Elizabethan compromise, although practical because of its flexibility, had left in its wake many serious Christians who yearned for a single focus and for wholehearted commitment.

Hooker was one of six children born to an independent farmer of Markfield, Leicestershire, in the heart of England. Little else is known about his childhood. He probably went to grammar school at Market Bosworth (where Samuel Johnson taught 125 years later). The task of a grammar school such as Hooker's was twofold. Boys between the ages of eight and fifteen were taught to read, write, and speak Latin and sometimes Greek. It was an exacting discipline, requiring thorough mastery of the language as well as saturation in the cadences of classical literature, attained through imitative writing. Equal emphasis if not equal time was attached to a complete grounding in the doctrine and practice of the Church of England. Of course all children had, from earliest childhood, absorbed a Christianity heavily laced with Calvinism, but in grammar school the tenets of the faith were given coherence and clarity.

In March of 1604 (one and a half years before Shepard was born), with his mind disciplined by the study of Latin and Greek and his heart filled with the rigors of Reformed theology, Hooker set off for Cambridge. Although his original destination was Queens College, he transferred—probably within the year—to Emmanuel College, which was also the college of Shepard, John Cotton, Thomas Weld, and Samuel Stone.

From the time of its founding, Emmanuel was widely known as a Puritan college. It was founded by Sir Walter Mildmay, who was Queen Elizabeth's Chancellor of the Exchequer. There is a story told by a contemporary historian which contains essential if not literal truth. The queen is said to have addressed her Chancellor:

> *"Sir Walter, I hear you have erected a Puritan foundation."*
>
> *"No Madam," saith he, "Far be it from me to countenance anything contrary to your established laws; but I have set an acorn, which when it becomes an oak, God alone knows what will be the fruit thereof.*[4]

Mildmay's purpose was to educate a preaching ministry, because he believed that inspired preaching was the key to the transformation of a lethargic church into a vital one. He chose as master Lawrence Chaderton, a learned theologian and convert from Roman Catholicism. Chaderton was a moving and powerful preacher, and he deplored the widespread ignorance and apathy among English parish priests. He was in complete accord with Mildmay's purpose, as he made clear in a sermon at St. Paul's Cross in 1578, before Emmanuel had been founded:

> *Where are the lips of those ministers which do preserve knowledge, or those messengers of God at whose mouths his poor people should seek his law? Nay, rather, where be not whole swarms of idle, ignorant, and ungodly curates and readers who neither can nor will go before the dear flock of Christ in soundness of doctrine and integrity of life. . . . What shall I say of our dumb dogs, non-residents and all those who serve mortal and sinful men with simony, flattering words and servile obedience.*[5]

Chaderton was filled with indignation, but he was also wise, flexible, and realistic—qualities that enabled him to guide Emmanuel College on an increasingly Puritan course without serious interference from the episcopal authorities.

The college chapel provided a noticeable architectural contrast to the other university chapels built in Gothic and Tudor styles and rich in colorful stained glass. Mildmay's chapel was startling in its simplicity and faced north and south instead of east and west, in defiance of orthodox Christian practice. The quiet, whitewashed interior, framed with heavy, dark beams was flooded with the light of day. No surplices or hoods were worn there. Departures from the Book of Common Prayer were numerous and thought by many to be radical. One observer was especially shocked at the manner in which communion was shared:

> They receive that holy sacrament, sitting about the communion table, and do pull the loaf one from the other, after the minister hath begun. And so the cup, one drinking as it were to another, like good fellows, without any particular application of the said words more than once for all.[6]

Extemporaneous prayers were even worse, said another observer: "We have such prayers of every man's own making (and sometimes sudden conceiving too) vented among us that besides the absurdities of the language directed to God himself our young scholars are thereby taught to prefer the private spirit before the public."[7]

Such revolutionary behavior was intended to simplify forms of worship in order to return to what was believed to have been the practice of the early church and also to eliminate whatever practices might be misconstrued by ignorant people as idolatrous. Forms of worship, for the Puritan leaders of Emmanuel, were to show forth the Spirit, unencumbered by the accretions of centuries of Roman Catholic imagination.

The intensity of the religious atmosphere at Emmanuel and its unfamiliar forms of worship gave the college a reputation among outsiders of being a rather dreary place, characterized by ostentatious religiosity and a kind of grim sincerity. Richard Corbett, a contemporary satirical poet, expressed what many others felt at the time in a poem called "The Distracted Puritan":

> In the house of pure Emmanuel
> I had my education;
> Where my friends surmise

I dazzled mine eyes
With the light of Revelation.

Refrain:
Boldly I preach, hate cross, hate a surplice,
Miters, copes and rotchets; *
Come hear me pray nine times a day,
And fill your head with crotchets. **8

*Episcopal vestment
**Whimsical fancies

Thomas Hooker remained at Emmanuel for fourteen years, receiving his bachelor of arts and master of arts degrees there, and then going on to be both Fellow and Catechist. He also became an accomplished preacher, eager to spread the saving news of the gospel. He left Emmanuel in 1618 to become the rector of St. George's Church in Esher, Surrey, and, more important for his ministry, chaplain in the household of one Francis Drake, the patron of the parish church in Esher and a large local landholder. As chaplain he was responsible in particular for the pastoral care of Joan Drake, the spiritually ailing wife of his patron. George H. Williams has pointed out the formative influence of this period of Hooker's life on his development as theologian and healer of souls, as he focused his attention on the dynamics of the conversion process in response to Mrs. Drake's needs.[9]

When he was called to Esher, Hooker was already known as a pastor who had himself been through a difficult conversion and had begun to use this experience in counseling others. The model for spiritual healing, which in those first years of ministry came from his own self-analysis, was in most respects similar to the morphology of conversion in which he had been educated. His experience had begun with an awareness of sin that had the violence of seizure. As Cotton Mather recounts it,

> *It pleased the Spirit of God very powerfully to break into his soul*
> *with such a sense of being exposed to the just wrath of heaven, as*
> *filled him with most unusual degrees of horror and anguish which*

broke not only his rest, but his heart also, and caused him to cry out, "While I suffer thy terrors, O Lord, I am distracted."

His expectation and his education told him that "there was no way but submission to God . . . but when he came to apply the rule unto himself . . . he could do nothing." Then (and this is the unusual aspect of Hooker's conversion) he began to meditate on the promises of God to the faithful, saying to himself as he lay down at night, "I will lay me down in peace and sleep; for thou, O Lord, makest me dwell in assurance."[10] When faith came to Hooker, it was not in the flash that he may have anticipated. Instead, his humble search for openness to God allowed him to enter quietly into the covenant.

His awareness that conversion can take many forms made Hooker particularly creative in his approach to the difficult conversion of Joan Drake. Hers was an illustrious case. Before Hooker was called to her, she had been counseled by nine other clerics, the last of whom was John Dod, identified by one scholar as perhaps "the chief holy man of the spiritual brotherhood."[11] It was Dod who suggested that Hooker, his junior colleague by thirty years, be called to Esher.

A contemporary account described Joan Drake as "a bright, responsive woman, with a quick sparrow-hawk eye, of a natural jovial constitution, accidently melancholy, full of love . . . with a deep and nimble quick, pleasant, present wit, tender-hearted, free and bountiful, in nothing covetous but grace."[12] However, following the birth of her third child and first daughter, she became depressed, changeable, discontented. She brooded over the state of her soul, convinced that her sin against the Holy Spirit was so serious as to be unpardonable. Feeling destined for damnation, she could not repent and turned instead to merrymaking; she did "not deny herself pleasures and jollity and mirth." In the presence of clergy she became unreachable and resentful. When John Dod tried to pray with her she mocked him: "Seeing you see what a wicked creature I am, why do you trouble yourself any more with me?" That prayerful session ended with her attempt to hit him over the head with a bedstaff.[13] Many times over, in despair, she tried to commit suicide.

Through many months, Hooker counseled Joan Drake with patience, sensitivity, and resourcefulness until, in an ecstatic experience, her conversion was accomplished. Her conversion as well as his prolonged intimate contact with her profoundly affected Hooker and shaped his ministry significantly. It gave him what we might today call "clinical experience" of what to look for in similar cases. He had observed, for example, that she kept grace away by her overscrupulousness as she searched and searched for sin. He saw her at other times thrashing about over the hopelessness of her situation, which led him to reflect on the evil of despair and later to preach that it "is as truly sin as... swearing, stealing, whoring or murder."[14] From Joan Drake he learned, too, to have greatly deepened sympathy for the suffering of those with spiritual illness and to address his message more than before to "poor doubting Christians." Finally, his success confirmed in him his vocation as a physician of the soul.

One other important change in Hooker's life resulted from his sojourn in Esher. There he met and married his wife. For a Puritan chaplain in a gentleman's household to marry a member of the entourage was by no means unusual. Thomas Shepard did the same thing, and so did Roger Williams. In fact, it was said of chaplains: "If they come single it's a thousand to one they will either be in love or married before they go away."[15] In the Drake household, Hooker met and married Susannah Garbrand, a woman in waiting to Joan Drake. Their first child, who was born there, was named Joanna after Joan Drake. This Joanna Hooker, when she had grown up and moved to Hartford, Connecticut, became Thomas Shepard's second wife and, upon her marriage, received a bequest from the will of the grateful Francis Drake.

From Esher, Hooker moved on to a wider world. He answered a call to Chelmsford in Essex to be lecturer and "assistant on the Lord's Days" at the Church of St. Mary. At forty he was at the height of his powers. The range and strength of his personality were soon acknowledged both by friends and foes around Chelmsford. As a preacher, it was said that by the authority of his bearing and the poignancy of his message he was able to turn mocking disbelievers into penitents. On one famous occasion, during a visit to his home in Leicestershire, one of the chief burgesses of the town tried to prevent him from preaching there in the great church. When he found himself unable to forestall Hooker, the burgess instead

> Set certain fiddlers at work to disturb him in the church-porch, but such was the vivacity of Mr. Hooker, as to proceed in what he was about, without either the changing of his mind, or the drowning of his voice; whereupon [one of the men] himself went unto the church door to overhear what he said.

Hooker's words got "first the attention and then the conviction of that wretched man."[16]

With increased public exposure and increased involvement in the politics of Puritanism, Hooker grew in stature as a Puritan activist during this period. He was dynamic and fearless, never awed by power in high places. He was, in fact, "a person who while doing the Lord's work would put a King in his pocket."

Hooker's greatest weakness was a violent temper. For the most part it was under good control, and, in fact, he used it effectively. It was observed that "He had as much government of his anger as a man with a mastiff dog in chain; he would let out his dog and pull in his dog as he pleased." But occasionally his anger overcame him, and he would on those occasions disarmingly and humbly acknowledge his error. He once accused a little boy of vandalism: "The boy denied it, and Mr. Hooker still went on in an angry manner. . . whereupon said the boy, 'Sir, I see you are in a passion, I'll say no more to you,' and so ran away." Hooker investigated the circumstances, found that the boy was telling the truth, and sent for him, saying: "Indeed I was in a passion, when I spake to you before; it was my sin, it is my shame and I am truly sorry for it; and I hope in God I shall be more watchful hereafter." The boy never forgot the encounter.[17]

The qualities that account for the preservation of the Hooker lore, his magnetism, his commanding presence, his passion close to the surface, his willing humility, were the qualities that, when exercised in the pulpit, made him the highly influential preacher and public figure he became in England and New England.

His preaching style was direct, simple, and sincere as well as very consciously crafted. He knew that changes of pace stirred crowds, and he believed in unleashing his passion at times, as he advised a young friend before a sermon: "Sym, let it be hot."[18] At other times Hooker could be quiet, analytical, and probing.

The message that he preached in Chelmsford was the central one of his career. He preached it three times over, in three sets of sermons, once at Emmanuel "in a more scholastic way," once at Chelmsford, "in a more popular way," and again in New England, where his transplanted Essex parishioners asked him "once more to go over the points of God's regenerating works upon the soul of the elect; until at last their desires prevailed with him to resume that pleasant subject."[19]

Hooker always began by addressing his parishioners where he found them, lost in the psychological and moral corruption they had inherited from their biblical parents. "My purpose," he said, "is not to begin with the knowledge of God but with the knowledge of ourselves because it is most available to make us see our misery and the need of a Saviour."[20] The task of the physician of the soul was first to awaken complacent or rebellious churchgoers to a vivid awareness of their corruption and need, and then, eventually, to lead the ones who had been chosen back into God's presence where they could become whole in divine love.

As he approached the healing process, Hooker proceeded from his careful knowledge of the anatomy of the soul. The soul was composed of three parts: understanding, will, and affections. The understanding receives and analyzes information, passing along a reasoned recommendation to the will, which either accepts or rejects it. The affections respond to the determination of the will with fear, love, hate, or desire, and action follows. In their state of perfect grace before the fall, Adam and Eve understood God's will for them; by their own wills they followed him; and through their affections they were moved in love toward obedience and perfect harmony. For their descendants after the fall, this natural order has been dislocated. Human beings often do not recognize God's will, or turn from a dim perception of it in fear, selfishness, or apathy. Therefore, they need a physician of the soul to prepare them for healing.

Hooker's goal as pastor was formulated and articulated in his English years. Using the tools of contemporary religious psychology, he would lead his parishioners through the necessary stages of preparatory experience so that when grace came to those whom God had chosen they could accept it, be justified, and walk in God's ways.

Hooker's particular version of the *ordo salutis* developed out of his own conversion experiences, out of his encounter with Joan Drake, and out of a long life of meditation and patient ministry. The experience might begin, he told a neighboring congregation in Essex, with a cry of the soul, a "godly sorrow and grief of heart for thy failings."[21] This attitude of mind, which he called "contrition," represented a confrontation with the law and a shocked recognition of sin. It would be followed by humiliation, which released the sinner from self-centeredness and pride. Humiliation (when it was true humiliation and not despair) was an "inward frame of heart" in which one could accept God's mercy. It could be preceded by intense emotional turmoil, as in Hooker's own experience, but its essential quality was to open the soul to the promise of love. And it was through this intimation of love that grace came: "The greatness of this mercy of God, being settled upon the heart, inflames it. This sweetness warms the heart, this freeness kindles the fire; and when the greatness of the freeness comes to be valued this sets the heart all upon fire."[22]

The transformation of personality that took place was deep and forever; and, no matter how much the physician of the soul might have guided the penitent along the way, it was the work of God alone. George H. Williams quotes a passage from one of Hooker's Essex sermons, dramatizing the transformation:

> As it is with the wheels of a clock that runs quite wrong. What must a man do to set this clock right again? He must first stop it that it run no longer wrong, and then turn it, and set the wheels right. Now all this while the clock is a patient, and the workman doth all. Secondly, when it is thus set right, then the workman puts the plummets and weights on it, and now the wheels can run of themselves by virtue of that poise and weight they have gotten—so that these two are plain different actions.

Just so is it with the frame of the soul, the will, and the affections, which are the wheels of this great and curious clock (the soul goes hell-way and sin-ward, and the will and the affections embrace nothing but hell and sin). Now to bring these into holy order the Lord must stop the soul, and that is done by the discovery of sin, and by this humiliation of heart. . . .

But now when the soul is set heaven-ward, and God justifies a poor sinner, and plucks him to himself by faith, and adopts him to be a child, then he too gives him of his spirit; and this is as the weight of the soul. Then by the power of that Spirit the soul is able to run right, and hath a principle of grace in it. [23]

Hooker's message had a powerful impact. Especially in and around Chelmsford, his ministry effected a deep change, one that would be significant for New England. A small group of his parishioners were so moved by his preaching and felt themselves to be so touched by the Spirit that they were drawn close together under his leadership to form a little church within the parish of St. Mary's. It was a church unrecognized from the outside and undefined within, but nonetheless a reality that could be described. John Eliot, who was Hooker's assistant in a school where he taught near Chelmsford and later the pastor in Roxbury, Massachusetts, wrote many years later about Hooker's little community: "I have known. . . a communion of Christians who held frequent communion together, used the censure of admonition yea and of excommunication, with much presence of Christ, only they had not officers nor sacraments." Here the intimacy and strict discipline of a congregational church without its outward organization was contained within a large and motley parish church to the end that "the holy saints who are called higher by the grace of Christ" may "enjoy together a more strict and select communion unto which they may gather together."[24] Hooker's community, like Cotton's in Lincolnshire, was one of the vibrant, little nuclear churches that were gathering here and there in England and would become the precursors of the gathered church in New England.

Hooker's influence on other members of the Puritan brotherhood was also profound. He was the center of a network of dissident clergy who met together regularly, sometimes in one parish, sometimes in another, in something of the style of the prophesyings of the Elizabethan era. These gatherings of clergy had two purposes. They provided support for the brethren in their work through "fasting and prayer and profitable conferences," and they acted as a kind of underground employment agency for Puritan preachers without pulpits. The result was that "godly ministers came to be here and there settled in several parts of the country."[25] As a result of their common purpose, their frequent association, and their solidarity in the face of increasing harassment, this circle of ministers developed a community spirit that strengthened their resolve and gave peace to their spirits. "We were an intimate society for many years," wrote one of them later, "we took sweet counsel together, and walked unto the house of God in company. . . . We oft breathed and poured out our souls together in prayer, fasting and conferences."[26]

Like the secret gathered churches that so many of them experienced in England, Hooker's informal association of Puritan clergy was a proving ground for the clerical leaders of New England. The young members of the clergy were the most powerfully influenced by these meetings under his guidance. A local informant of Archbishop Laud wrote in a report to him, after investigating Hooker's subversive activities, that there were "divers young ministers about us that seldom study but spend their time in private meetings and conference with him . . . and return home in the end of the week and broach on the Sundays what he hath brewed."[27] Three of the most devoted of these young disciples were John Eliot, soon to be of Roxbury; Samuel Stone, who came to New England with Hooker; and Thomas Shepard.

Thomas Shepard: Towcester, Cambridge, Essex, Yorkshire, Northumberland

Thomas Shepard, uniquely among the Puritan divines of New England, left us an extensive legacy of personal information. His autobiography and journal make it possible for us to reconstruct a portrait of great interest and, in addition, provide us with illuminating insights into the evolution of Puritanism.

On Guy Fawkes Day, November 5, 1605, "at that very hour wherein the Parliament should have been blown up by Popish priests," Shepard was born in the town of Towcester, Northamptonshire, on the banks of the River Tove. Accordingly, he was named Thomas for the doubter, because, said his father, "I would hardly believe that ever any such wickedness should be attempted by men against so religious and good [a] Parliament."[28]

As he tells his story, several circumstances in Shepard's childhood are recalled with such emotion and such clarity as to indicate their formative influence in his life. One was the upward mobility of the breadwinners in his family from illiterate yeoman farmer to prosperous merchant to cultivated Master of Arts in three generations. His paternal grandfather, John Shepard, lived and farmed in the neighboring town of Foscote, where he made a good living but had little or no education. His grandson was ashamed of him on that account, describing his grandparents as "very well to live but very ignorant" (40). John Shepard's will was written by a scribe and signed with an X. Thomas Shepard's father, William Shepard, found his way off the farm by being apprenticed to a Towcester grocer named Bland. He eventually married the grocer's daughter, Anne, and not only learned to read and write but also became a well-to-do merchant and leader in civic affairs.[29] He was elected several times to the directorship of an endowment called the Sponne Charity, which disbursed funds for the town free school, for poor relief, and for road repair.[30] Shepard was proud of his father, describing him as "a wise and prudent man, the peacemaker of the place, and toward his latter end much blessed of God in his estate" (40). Thomas Shepard, the youngest son of the third generation, with the help and encouragement of his older brother, John, went off to Cambridge to become a highly educated clergyman. This kind of rapid social advancement can be difficult to absorb, especially in a setting in which values are rooted in generations of an essentially unchanging way of life. A measure of unsureness about personal identity and about the application of old values to new situations probably colored Shepard's life.

His experience of religious instability from the very beginning of life was also unsettling. The vicar at the church of St. Lawrence in Towcester, where the Shepards were baptized, married, and buried, was an orthodox priest of the Church of England named Francis Bradley. Towcester, however, is situated midway between Northampton and Banbury, both thriving market towns with strong Puritan ministries. William Shepard, who traveled about a lot marketing his wares, was influenced by the preaching he heard on his journeys. He became dissatisfied with the preaching of Francis Bradley and came to prefer the "stirring ministry" (40) of William Whately, the Puritan preacher at the church of St. Mary the Virgin in Banbury, known by some as the "roaring boy of Banbury."[31] William Shepard even bought a second house in Banbury and thought of moving there, so eager was he to hear the message preached there.

Shepard's mother, Anne, was also deeply devout. He described her as "much afflicted in conscience, sometimes even unto distraction of mind" (40). Shepard, therefore, from earliest childhood was exposed to the traditional worship of the Church of England, when he went to church and to school, and to a Puritanism at home which was intense and emotional by contrast.

A third and by far the most troubling circumstance in Shepard's youth was his turbulent family life. His account of his early years is tinged throughout with longing for a love that he could count on, that would enfold him with security. He was the youngest of nine children and his mother's "best beloved." She was a parent who, he remembered, "did bear exceeding love for me and made many prayers for me" (40). When he was very little, an epidemic struck the town, and Shepard was sent away to his grandparents' home, where he felt "much neglected of them." When he finally returned home, it was to a greatly changed household. His mother had died, and the epidemic had "swept away both sisters and servants." Hardest of all was his father's remarriage, which occurred either before his return or soon after, to a widow named Amy West. She brought two children to her new marriage and bore two more by William—Samuel, who came to New England with Shepard, and Elizabeth. Shepard longed for his own mother. Amy Shepard "did not seem to love me," he mourned, and she "let me see the difference between my own mother and a stepmother." Not only that, she also came between Thomas and his father and "incensed my father often against me." William, probably harassed by the discord in his home, was unwilling to take sides with his son against his new wife. Thomas was hurt and confused, probably tearful and difficult. He says, sadly, that he may even have deserved chastisement "justly also for my childishness" (40). Then his father fell ill, and Thomas was gripped by a terrible fear that he would be left "fatherless and motherless." He prayed "strongly and heartily for the life of my father... knowing I should be left alone if he was gone" (41). But his prayers were to no avail: "my father also died and also forsook me" (74).

Shepard's childhood trials were translated in maturity into an element in his deep and unusual spirituality. His acute longing for lost parents probably contributed to the yearning for direct communication with God, which breaks out clearly in his journal and underlies much of his thought. The loss of his parents, which he experienced as abandonment and total loss of control over his life, may have left him with a permanent unease, an inability ever completely to trust God, as well as a fierce rigidity by means of which he struggled to make his faith and his life predictable.

Soon after the death of his father, a new stability came into Shepard's life. He lived miserably in the household of Amy Shepard for only a short time and was then adopted by his older brother John and his wife. They took generous and good care of him. Their kindness and the special attention of William Cluer, a new schoolmaster at the Towcester Free School, pulled Shepard's life together. Cluer, an Emmanuel College graduate, inspired him to become a serious scholar and stirred his ambition to study for the ministry.

Thanks to the generosity and care of his brother, Shepard was able in February of 1620 to set out for Emmanuel College, at the age of fourteen—not unusually young for his time. At this openly Puritan college, Shepard, like Hooker, was exposed to and soon espoused an intense spiritual commitment and a liking for simplified worship. By

Shepard's time, however (fifteen years after Hooker's matriculation), there was also an increasing intellectual ferment in the society that reached him at Cambridge and unsettled him.

One element in the unrest was the continued fragmentation of organized religion. As each new fragment claimed the truth for itself, the question of the validity of any absolute truth arose in the minds of some. Although science was not yet a university discipline at Cambridge, scientific information generated at Gresham College in London and to some degree at Oxford circulated there, raising other questions. Galileo's discoveries reinforcing Copernican principles began to worry some of those who had linked the earth-centered Ptolemaic universe to an absolute God. And Francis Bacon's insistent advocacy of reasoning based on experimental evidence as a method that would make it possible "to examine and dissect the nature of the very world itself," undermined a widespread reverence for ancient authority. Those who would truly pursue knowledge, said William Harvey in the same vein, must "suffer not themselves to become enslaved and lose their freedom in bondage to the traditions and precepts of any, except their own eyes convince them."[32]

Some reacted with exhilaration to the ferment; these included Bacon himself and Thomas Hobbes, who was so entranced when he came upon the theorems of Euclid that "this made him in love with geometry," and thereafter he was even "wont to draw lines on his thigh and on the sheets, abed," according to a contemporary.[33] Others were deeply troubled by what appeared to be the disappearance of certitude, leaving "the imagination in a thousand labyrinths. What is all we know compared with what we know not?" asked William Drummond in his meditation on death.[34]

Just how far the new ideas of science and philosophy reached into Shepard's world he does not tell us. What we do know is that he was carried away by the excitement of unaccustomed intellectual delights when he first arrived in Cambridge and that the experience was followed by a period of relativistic doubt. He was especially intoxicated by the delights of the profane world outside Emmanuel. He took great pleasure in study, which led him, he said in retrospect, "to be foolish and proud and to show myself in the public schools [where debates and lectures were held for students from all colleges] and there to be a disputer about things which now I see I did not know then at all but only prated about them" (42). Caught up in the swirl of new ideas, Shepard began to lose his hold on the one absolute truth. In a remarkably modern passage, he describes the experience:

> *I felt all manner of temptations to all kind of religions, not knowing which I should choose, whether education might not make me believe what I had believed, and whether if I had been educated up among Papists I should not have been as verily persuaded that Popery is the truth or Turkism is the truth. (44)*

It was not, however, just the delights of learning that intoxicated Shepard. He also took to carousing with the new, sophisticated companions he had met outside of Emmanuel. Again in self-critical retrospect, he describes his behavior:

> *I came to dispute in the schools and there to join to loose scholars of other colleges and was fearfully left of God and fell to drink with them. And I drank so much one day that I was dead drunk, and that upon a Saturday night, and so was carried from the place I had drink at and did feast at unto a scholar's chamber . . . and knew not where I was until I awakened late on that Sabbath and sick with my beastly carriage. And when I awakened I . . . went out into the fields and there spent that Sabbath lying hid in the cornfields. (43)*

The conflicting influences and emotions bombarding his inner and outer consciousness had made Shepard's world chaotic. The old longing for absolute acceptance and perfect love still lingered in his mind, and now it combined with a new and urgent need to straighten out the turmoil in his present life. Such yearning for order and peace made him open and ready to hear the message of the spiritual preachers at Emmanuel and to follow them to conversion.

It was John Preston, successor to Laurence Chaderton as Master of the College, who reached Shepard at the crucial juncture. Preston spoke about the deep transformation that comes with spiritual rebirth, which "puts not upon us only the washy color of a good profession, but that dyes the heart in grain, . . . changeth the whole frame of the heart, . . . turns the rudder of life, and guides the course to quite a contrary point of the compass."[35]

When Preston preached in this vein to the students at Emmanuel, Shepard responded with all the enthusiasm and gratitude of a searching adolescent:

> The Lord so bored my ears as that I understood what he spake and the secrets of my soul were laid. . . [open] before me . . . as if one had told him of all that ever I did, of all the turning and deceits of my heart, insomuch as that I thought he was the most searching preacher in the world. And I began to love him much and to bless God. (44)

The conversion that followed remained vivid in Shepard's memory, occupying the longest single section of his autobiography. His conversion fitted into the general frame of the classical *ordo salutis* with, however, some significant differences. It began with the sharp awareness or "conviction" of sin. This came upon him in the cornfields after his night of carousing. It was an awareness that was primarily an intellectual recognition of a particular misdeed. "Although I was troubled for this sin," he tells us, "I did not know my sinful nature all this while" (43). Then Shepard, unlike Hooker, experienced a second step in the conversion process, which he later identified as "compunction," the emotional realization and complete comprehension of himself as sinner, separated from God. The sermon by Preston that "so bored [his] ears as that [he] understood," brought him thus far.

For months after he had learned to feel compunction, Shepard struggled with doubt, on the edge of despair, fearing that he had "committed the impardonable sin." He thought of suicide as "the terrors of God began to break in like floods of fire into my soul" (45).

Then one evening, quietly he realized that he could "do as Christ: when he was in agony he prayed earnestly." So doing, he found the way to let go, to turn himself over to God in complete humility: "to leave myself with him to do with me what he would, and then and never until then I found rest... and the terrors of the Lord began to assuage sweetly" (45–46). He had reached the humiliation that opens the soul to grace.

The story of Shepard's conversion is one of spiritual adventure; of scaling heights and falling into depths; of temptations, resistance, and complacency overcome. With one temptation, however, he was never able to deal definitively. This was the hope for an experience of perfect and blissful union with God in this life, which he encountered early in his conversion pilgrimage in the message of the antinomian preacher, Roger Brierly of Grindleton in Yorkshire: "I heard of Grindleton, and I did question whether that glorious state of perfection might not be the truth" (44–45).[36] The message appealed to the longing in Shepard's heart for absolute assurance, and it lingered there, imperfectly suppressed for the rest of his life. One scholar suggests that Shepard's implacable opposition to Anne Hutchinson—who, as we have seen, preached a similar message in New England—sprang from his fear of that old yearning. As late as 1642, he confessed to his journal the temptation he felt, "to forsake the scriptures and wait for a spirit to suggest immediately God's inmost thought toward me" (112).[37] Shepard himself, of course, made no such connection between his adolescent and adult spirituality. For him, his youthful antinomian stirrings were one more temptation successfully defeated.

Shepard's conversion experience was for him a single powerful ray, which illuminated both his personality and his vocation for the rest of his life. At the same time that it satisfied his deepest desires and gave order to his life, it became, as Hooker's conversion had for him, the stuff of which his ministry was made, providing him with insights that he would use to bring other souls to Christ as well as a prototype for subsequent preaching and counseling. Since the experience was very different for the two men, however, it produced different effects in their ministries. Although he had his own protracted struggle with the law, Hooker eventually found his way to God by meditating on the loving promises God offers to the faithful, and he experienced grace in quiet stirrings, gradually. Shepard, on the other hand, felt deeply that a radical self-confrontation resulting in complete emptying of the self in humiliation had, for him, been a necessary part of the approach to God. Openness to God's love, he believed, could come only with total surrender. When he came to apply his own experience to the healing of souls, therefore, Shepard's method as a physician proved to be far more surgical than Hooker's.

After his conversion, Shepard pursued his studies with increasingly focused diligence. In 1627 he received his Master of Arts degree from Emmanuel College and at twenty-two went out to take up his first employment, feeling grateful for his calling but "young and weak and unexperienced and unfit for so great a work" (49).

His first pastorate followed from an undergraduate apprenticeship he had held in Terling in the Essex parish of Thomas Weld, later pastor of the church in Roxbury in the Bay Colony. In Terling, Shepard had participated in the ministers' association of which Hooker was the center, and there his long and fond acquaintance with Hooker began. Hooker took a fatherly interest in him at once, aiding Shepard in his search for employment but cautioning the young man against taking the first available opportunity offered him in the Essex town of Coggeshall. As Shepard recounts the story,

> Mr. Hooker . . . did object against my going thither for being but young and unexperienced, and there being an old yet sly and malicious minister in the town . . . did therefore say it was dangerous and uncomfortable for little birds to build under the nests of old ravens and kites. (48)

Eventually, on the advice of Hooker and his associates, Shepard accepted a lectureship endowed by a Puritan benefactor in the town of Earles Colne in northern Essex.

From tentative beginnings, Shepard gained confidence as a pastor in Earles Colne. "I found the Lord putting forth his strength in my extreme weakness and not forsaking me when I was so foolish," he said of those earliest days of ministry (50). As he gained confidence, Shepard began in Earles Colne to preach the message that he would prune and shape for the rest of his career. Its core changed very little over the years, but his approach varied a great deal in response to the circumstances of his life and the needs of the congregations to whom he ministered. As he fled from church authorities northward to Yorkshire, Northumberland, and finally to New England, he was forced to confront widely disparate social and ecclesiastical conditions, which led him to adapt his style and emphasis in order to reach different people in different situations. But the essential message and method remained the one he formulated at Earles Colne: "The course I took in my preaching was (1) to show the people their misery; (2) the remedy, Christ Jesus; (3) how they should walk answerable to this mercy, being redeemed by Christ"(50).

That he was successful we know from his own account of the devoted followers who gathered around him after the time of his lectureship had expired and who asked him to stay on. We know of his success, too, from the attention he received from the ecclesiastical authorities, which forced him to flee northward to a chaplaincy in Yorkshire and finally to a little town near Newcastle called Heddon-on-the-Wall.

It was at Heddon that Shepard's earliest surviving sermons were preached; they clearly reflect the circumstances of the parish in which he found himself, a situation very different from the Essex where Hooker had fashioned his message and where Shepard had begun to preach. Northumberland was remote, largely unpenetrated by Reformation doctrine or practice, and far beyond the Church of England's reach to enforce effectively any sort of uniformity. Although officially forbidden, Roman Catholicism was still widespread there. Rural populations were poor and illiterate, congregations inattentive, boisterous, and irreverent. One account describes a local churchgoing scene: "Holy communion is but administered once in the year. On these occasions when five or six hundred souls come forward at once there was such pushing and shoving, such a confusion and noise that oftentimes the young and old people are carried down with the crowding."[38]

Shepard's predecessor at Heddon had been a rowdy, cocksure curate, son of a country squire and frequently "merry with drink."[39] Although Shepard had preached to a mixed audience of country and gentlefolk in Essex, it had been the gentlefolk who tended to gather around him. He was shocked and awed by what he saw of the country folk in his new congregation. In outrage, he addressed his flock: "Look up and down the kingdom, you shall see some roaring, drinking, dining, carding, whoring, in taverns and blind alehouses; others belching out their oaths, their mouths even casting out like raging seas, filthy, frothy speeches."[40]

The style of Shepard's preaching in Northumberland was the result of his sense of urgency. He believed with all his heart that his message was a life-and-death matter. He wanted to capture the people he could reach in his unruly congregation and shake them into recognizing their need for healing. He spoke with passion, seeking to call people out from a way of life that was leading them headlong to eternal death.

The sermons he preached were part of a series designed to lead would-be believers to conversion through an analysis of nine principles of faith. The first six, a call to conversion, were completed in Northumberland and later published as the *Sincere Convert*. The remaining three, dealing with the conversion process, were preached in New England and published as the *Sound Believer*. The English sermons developed the objectives of Shepard's Essex years in much more extended and dramatic form. He set out to show his congregation "the bottomless gulf of sin and misery" that was the natural condition of fallen humankind and to offer "the Lord Jesus Christ [as] the only means of redemption," sharpening the message with the warning that "those that are saved out of this woeful estate . . . are very few."[41]

The series begins with an evocation of the glory and "all-sufficiency of God:

> O, pass by all the rivers, till thou come to the spring head; wade
> through all creatures, till thou art drowned, plunged and swal-
> lowed up with God. When thou seest the heavens, say, Where is
> that great Builder that made this? . . . When thou tastest sweet-

ness in the creature or in God's ordinances, say, Where is sweetness itself, beauty itself? Where is the sea of these drops, the sun of these beams?[42]

The glory of this God was reflected in his creation. Adam "when he came first out of God's mint shined most glorious," and "God did most dearly love him." The Creator and his creation were bound together in love: "Methinks I see Adam rapt up in continual ecstacies in having this God."[43]

The fall meant separation, the end of God's love, the end of tranquillity: "Man is now rejected of God that was beloved of God. He is now runagate all up and down the earth that once was prince and Lord of all the world."[44] The imputation of Adam's sin to humankind meant a radical transformation of character as well:

> *Every natural man and woman is born full of all sin, as full as a toad is of poison, as full as ever his skin can hold; . . . thy mind is a nest of all the foul opinions, heresies, that were ever vented by any man; thy heart is a foul sink of all atheism, sodomy, blasphemy, whoredom, adultery, witchcraft, buggary; so that, if thou hast any good thing in thee, it is as a drop of rosewater in a bowl of poison; where fallen it is all corrupted.*[45]

The ultimate consequence of corruption is everlasting torment of body and mind: "Thou canst not endure the torments of a little kitchen fire on the tip of thy finger, not one half hour together. How wilt thou bear the fury of this infinite, endless, consuming fire in body and soul throughout all eternity." Torment of mind produces the ultimate anguish: "A guilty conscience shall torment thee as if thou hadst swallowed down a living poisonful snake which shall lie gnawing and biting thine heart for sin past, day and night."[46] In a passage unusual even among the most austere of Puritan orators, Shepard then speaks unequivocally about election, thus enormously magnifying the fearful tension he has already carefully built:

It is a thousand to one if ever thou be one of that small number whom God hath picked out to escape this wrath to come. . . . It is true, Christ spent not his breath to pray for all . . . much less his blood for all; therefore, he was never intended as a redeemer for all.[47]

Finally, when there is no longer anywhere to turn, Shepard opens up the only possible avenue for the sinner to rush into: "Cast thyself into the arms of Christ, and if thou perish, perish there."[48]

Shepard's Northumberland call is to valor, daring, endurance, and ultimate surrender: "O strive then to be one of them that shall be saved, though it cost thee thy blood and the loss of all that thou hast. . . . Venture, at least, and try what the Lord will do for thee."[49] It was a stirring call, the kind of call that would be echoed around England as the "revolution of the saints" approached.[50]

It was not until Shepard reached New England, where his circumstances and his audience were very different, that we can more than glimpse the warmer spirituality that he allowed to break forth there.[51] And not until his New England sermons will we find a more generous sympathy with suffering souls, as he gradually became a more gentle physician.

3

THE CALL TO NEW ENGLAND

Thomas Hooker, Samuel Stone, and the Braintree Company

The story of the call to New England for each of the Puritan divines who emigrated was, as we have seen, also the story of the deepening crisis within the Church of England. The gradually mounting pressure to conform and a corresponding stiffening of resistance on the part of the Puritan clergy are clearly evident in the story of the last English years of the founders of the Church of Christ in Cambridge.

For nearly four years after assuming his position as Lecturer and "assistant on the Lord's Days" at St. Mary's Church in Chelmsford, Thomas Hooker was not seriously disturbed by church authorities. Although not otherwise identifiable as a Puritan, the rector of the parish, John Michaelson, was an appointee of the Puritan family of Mildmay and was committed to the ideal of a preaching ministry. He, therefore, "gladly encouraged Mr. Hooker and lived with him in a most comfortable amity."[1] Hooker flourished in the relative freedom to develop his powers. During those years he established his reputation as a gifted teacher and healer of souls, and he earned the respect of a wide circle of clergy on both sides of the Puritan question. However, when William Laud became Bishop of London in 1628, attention was immediately focused on Hooker as a man to be carefully watched because of the suspicious nature of both his position and his activities.

The very fact that he was a lecturer rather than a beneficed clergyman was in itself suspicious because lecturers were usually outside of episcopal control, being supported by private endowment—often, as in this case, by Puritan endowment. In addition, he was a preacher with enormous influence which extended well beyond Chelmsford and drew off the congregations of other, more conservative preachers. He was also, as we have seen, the leader of a clerical association that met together monthly for worship, mutual support, and the maintenance of an underground Puritan network. Finally, and most irritating of all to the Bishop, Hooker had openly criticized him for his suppression of a preaching ministry and for his promotion of high church doctrine.

In the spring of 1629 a summons from the Court of High Commission, the highest ecclesiastical court, was imminent. At this juncture the wise and moderate vicar of nearby Braintree, one Samuel Collins, wrote to Laud advising caution in proceeding against Hooker because of the enormous influence he was believed to have. Collins spoke of popular "palates that grow so out of taste that no food contents them but of Mr. Hooker's dressing," and of the young clergy who "spend their time in private meetings and conference with him. . . . He is their oracle in cases of conscience and points of divinity and their principle library."[2] He warned that popular interest in Hooker's plight was running high: "All men's heads tongues, eyes and ears are . . . taken up with plotting, talking, and expecting what will be the conclusion of Mr. Hooker's business."[3] Collins advised Laud to "connive at Mr. Hooker's departure" rather than to proceed against him, with the idea that without a confrontation "our people would soon be weaned from him and gained to their own pastors again."[4] The upshot was that Hooker was summoned to appear before Laud in London, probably in June, where he was warned to mend his ways but not suspended.

The mounting tension clearly unsettled Hooker since during these same months of 1629 he began to consider an alternative to resistance. On March 4 a charter had been granted to the Massachusetts Bay Company, and by summer specific plans for the plantation of a colony were being formulated. In mid-July, Hooker, Roger Williams (then chaplain to a Puritan nobleman in Essex), and John Cotton rode together to Sempringham Castle in Lincolnshire, seat of Theo-philous Clinton, Earl of Lincoln.[5] There on July 25 they met with some members of the Massachusetts Bay Company and their elected governor, John Winthrop, to formulate definite plans for the colony and for the departure of a party to New England the following March 11. Hooker, although vitally interested in the emigration, decided to persevere for the moment in his English ministry and returned home to Chelmsford to continue on his uncompromising course.

He was soon in trouble again because he could not and would not let his evangelism go. One local vicar, who was one of those suffering from the drain on his parish caused by the charismatic, nonconform-ing preaching of Hooker, was particularly outraged at the injustice be-ing done to himself and other conforming clergy. He wrote to Laud that Hooker, far from changing his ways as he had been admonished to do, "doth . . . continue in his former practices," and that local con-gregations have become "overmuch addicted to hearing the Word (as they call it) even to the neglect of God's holy and divine service and worship."[6]

There were petitions against Hooker, and petitions in support of him circulated among the clergy of Essex. By February of 1630, he had been deprived of his lectureship and had left Chelmsford to retire to his home called Cuckoos Farm in nearby Little Baddow. There, with John Eliot as his assistant, he opened a school. And there, from his home, he continued to preach, to hold his monthly meetings with the clergy, and unremittingly to fray the nerves of his bishop. The provo-cation soon proved too much for Laud. Hooker was cited to appear be-fore the Court of High Commission. Rather than appear, he once again considered going to New England, but in the end decided on flight to the Netherlands. He left his wife and five children under the protection of his Emmanuel College friend and patron, Robert Rich, Earl of Warwick, at Rich's estate in Great Waltham. On the eve of his departure, perhaps on Maundy Thursday, April 17, 1631, Hooker preached a farewell sermon to friends and parishioners. It is filled with the urgency and the sense of doom that increasingly hung over Puri-tans in those dark days:

*I will deal plainly with you, as sure as God is God, God is going
from England. . . for England hath seen her best days and the re-
ward of sin is coming on apace; for God is packing up his gospel,
because none will buy his words. . . . Oh, therefore, my
brethren, lay hold on God, let him not go out of your coasts.
(He is going!) Look about you, I say, and stop him at the town's
end, and let not thy God depart. . . . Suffer him not to go far,
suffer him not to say farewell, or rather fare-ill England.* [7]

Hooker boarded a ship bound for the Netherlands in late spring
with Laud's henchmen in hot pursuit. Miraculously, the story goes,
just as he hopped on board, the wind sprang up "fair and fresh . . . and
he was no sooner under sail but the officer arrived at the seaside, hap-
pily too late now to come at him." [8]

His sojourn in Holland provided Hooker neither with circumstances in which he could exercise his gifts with real freedom and creativity nor with an atmosphere in which he could build a church
according to the pure form for which he now longed. The call he first
received from the English church in Amsterdam to serve as assistant to
the pastor, John Paget, never materialized because of Paget's own opposition to Hooker's radical congregationalism. From Amsterdam he
went to Delft, where he became assistant to the Scottish pastor, John
Forbes. They got along well together, having, it was said, "one soul in
two bodies." [9] Whatever the truth of that statement, his relationship
with Forbes was not by itself nearly enough to give Hooker real peace
of mind and spirit. In the eighteen months that he served in Delft he
was always restless, plagued by a sense of the fruitlessness of his mission, by his long absence from his family, and eventually by illness as
well. In the spring of 1633 he wrote to John Cotton in an exceedingly
downcast mood, in marked contrast to the zest and fire of his usual
style:

*The state of these Provinces to my weak eye seems wonderfully
ticklish and miserable. For the better part [with respect to] heart
religion they content themselves with very forms though much*

blemished; but the power of godliness, for aught I can see or hear, they know not. And if it [heart religion] were thoroughly pressed, I fear lest it will be fiercely opposed. My ague yet holds me. The ways of God's providence, wherein he has walked toward me, in this long time of my sickness, and wherein I have drawn forth many wearyish hours under his almighty hand (blessed be his name) together with pursuits and banishment, which have waited upon me, as one wave follows another, have driven me to an amazement, his paths being too secret and past finding out by such an ignorant, worthless worm as myself. I have looked over my heart and life according to my measure, aimed and guessed as well as I could, and entreated his Majesty to make known his mind, wherein I missed. And yet methinks I cannot spell out readily the purpose of his proceedings, which, I confess have been wonderful in miseries and more than wonderful in mercies to me and mine. [10]

Shortly after writing this letter Hooker returned to England, finally determined to accede to the wishes of the party of friends and parishioners who had already gone ahead to New England in the hope that he would follow them and become their pastor. This group was made up of Hooker's followers from the vicinity of Braintree, just north of Chelmsford, and was known as the Braintree Company. Its members organized themselves some time after Hooker's departure for the Netherlands and formulated a plan to emigrate. In 1632 or even late 1631, one part of the company settled at Mt. Wollaston in present-day Quincy before moving on to Cambridge, as John Winthrop noted in his *Journal* under the date August 14, 1632: "The Braintree Company (which had begun to sit down at Mt. Wollaston)... removed to Newtown. These were Mr. Hooker's Company." [11] Another group of passengers from the same area arrived in Boston on the ship *Lyon* on September 16, 1632, and went straight to Newtown. Still other friends and parishioners filtered into Newtown in smaller groups. From passenger lists, land grant records, the roll of men admitted to the General Court as freemen, and the confessions made by three of the group when they joined Shepard's church some years later, we know most of their names and something of their origins. Among them were John Bridge, whose statue stands on the Cambridge Common today and who would soon write to Shepard urging him to emigrate, and William Goodwin, soon to become ruling elder.

Joining with the small group of settlers from Boston who were already there, the members of the Braintree Company with Bridge and Goodwin as their leaders built the "first house for public worship at Newtown . . . with a bell upon it" at the corner of the present Dunster and Mt. Auburn Streets.[12] They had brought the bell with them from England and almost certainly carried it off to Hartford in the Hooker migration of 1636. At least, for a decade thereafter there is no mention of a bell in Newtown, parishioners being called to worship by the beating of a drum instead. The early records of Hartford, however, do attest to a bell. The legend in Hartford today, is, in fact, that the present bell of the First Church of Christ (Center Church) was cast from the remains of that early one.

In the new four-square, frame meetinghouse probably late in 1632, the first church in Newtown was gathered, an event commemorated at Center Church, Hartford, in 1982 as the anniversary of its founding. As in the early days in Plymouth, they had no pastor, but a pastor was not necessary to the gathering of a church. Only a community of the faithful with the will and the call to covenant together was needed, and that they had. As a covenanted community they constituted themselves a Church of Christ with all the powers of admission, dismissal, and discipline as well as the power to choose and ordain officers. William Goodwin was elected ruling elder, as was possibly also Andrew Warner. John Bridge may have been elected deacon then, as well. Goodwin had no authority to administer the sacraments but, like William Brewster in Plymouth, probably preached every Sunday and conducted worship according to what was gradually becoming an established order: an opening prayer, a sung Psalm, Old and New Testament readings, a sermon, another sung Psalm, an offering, and a final blessing.

Another part of the Braintree Company seems to have remained in

IRISH SEA

NORTH SEA

HADRIAN'S WALL

NEWCASTLE

HEDDON-ON-THE-WALL

BUTTERCRAMBE

YORK

ALFORD

BOSTON

MARKFIELD

SEMPRINGHAM CASTLE

MARKET BOSWORTH

CAMBRIDGE

TOWCESTER

EARLS COLNE

BANBURY

BRAINTREE

KELVEDON

TERLING

CHELMSFORD

LONDON

ESHER

ENGLISH CHANNEL

1. *The English heritage of the First Church in Cambridge—points of special interest. Map of England drawn by Julia C. Drinker.*

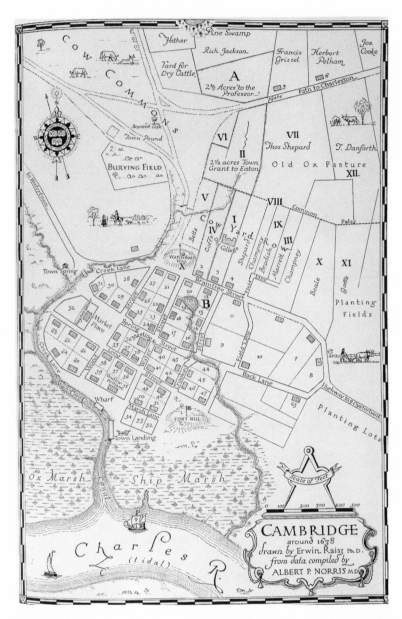

2. *Map of early Cambridge. Drawn by Edwin Raisz, Ph.D., from data compiled by Albert P. Norris, M.D., and prepared at the Institute of Geographical Exploration. Published in* Founding of Harvard College *by Samuel Eliot Morison, Cambridge, Mass.: Harvard University Press. Copyright 1935 by the President and Fellows of Harvard College. Copyright © renewed 1963 by Samuel Eliot Morison.*

3. Statue of John Bridge on the Cambridge Common. Sculpture by Thomas R. Gould, completed by Marshall S. Gould, 1882. Photograph by Stephen Ferry/Gamma Liaison.

4. "To my deare son Thomas Shepard": dedication of Thomas Shepard's Autobiography to his son. Published by permission of the First Church in Cambridge, Congregational, U.C.C., and the Houghton Library, Harvard University, bMS AM 1671 (1).

the house of mr Cottington being
forsaken at that time, & that it
much loved;

When we had bin here 2 dayes vpõ the
munday oct: 5: we came (being sent
for by freinds at Newtown) to them
to my brother mr Stons house; & that
cougregatiõ being vpon theire remouall
to Hartford at Conecticut my selfe
& those that came with me found
many houses empty & many of our willing
to sell; & heare of company bought
off theire houses to dwell in vntill
we should see another place fit to
remoue vnto, but hauing bin
here some time diuorse of our
brethren did desire to sit still
& not to remoue farther partly
because of the fellowship of the
churches partly ble they thought theire
liues were short & remoouall
to new plantatiom full of troubles
partly because they found sufficient
for themselues & theire company; here vpon
there was a purpose to enter into
church fellowship wch we did, the
yeare after about — the end
of the winter: a fortnight after wch
my deare wife Margaret dyed
being first received into church
fellowship, which as shee made longer
for so the Lord did so sweeten it
vnto her, that shee was hereby

6. *House in Cambridge occupied in succession by Thomas Hooker, Thomas Shepard, and Jonathan Mitchel. Sketch from memory after its demolition (1844), in* Harvard Book, II, 22. *Published in* Founding of Harvard College *by Samuel Eliot Morison, Cambridge, Mass.: Harvard University Press. Copyright 1935 by the President and Fellows of Harvard College. Copyright © renewed 1963 by Samuel Eliot Morison.*

7. *Fourth meetinghouse of the First Church in Cambridge, 1757–1833. Lithograph published in* Lectures on the History of the First Church in Cambridge *by Alexander McKenzie, Boston, Mass.: Congregational Publishing Society, 1873.*

8. Shepard Memorial Church, the sixth meetinghouse of the First Church in Cambridge, Congregational, U.C.C. Drawing by Abel C. Martin, architect, in 1870 for church dedicated in 1872. Published by permission of the First Church in Cambridge, Congregational, U.C.C.

9. *The First Church in Cambridge, Congregational, U.C.C., sixth meetinghouse. Drawing by Perry K. Neubauer, 1995.*

10. *The First Church in Cambridge, Unitarian Universalist. Drawing by Perry K. Neubauer, 1995.*

England, where its members communicated with Hooker in the Netherlands and apparently made the arrangements for an assistant to go with him to New England. According to Cotton Mather, Hooker's first choice was John Cotton, who declined. The company then asked John Norton, who came later to New England to be the pastor at Ipswich and Boston. Then, apparently Thomas Shepard was approached, although strangely there is no report of such an overture in the Shepard records. Finally, the choice fell on Samuel Stone, who accepted.[13]

Stone's education and English experience suited him admirably for the New England mission, both as pastor and as a colleague of other Puritan leaders. He was born in Hertford, just west of Essex, in 1602, the son of a John Stone. He was nearly eighteen when he entered Emmanuel College and very soon met Thomas Shepard, who became his lifelong friend. In Shepard's carousing days, Stone, who was three years older, was a steadying and comforting influence. As earnest undergraduates, they would sit by the fire together and talk about the presence of God in their lives and the alternative before them in the flames of the fire (74–75).

Stone took his Bachelor of Arts with Shepard in 1624 and then went on to study at Ashen on the edge of Suffolk County with Richard Blacerby (or Blackerby), a Puritan theologian and pastoral counselor who remained unordained because of his reluctance to accept episcopal ordination. He did, however, take in young clergymen for postgraduate studies. Subsequently, at about the same time that Shepard received his first position in Earles Colne in 1627, Stone accepted his first appointment as curate in Stisted, a town six miles to the south. During those years, both young men sat at the feet of Hooker and became intimately connected with the underground network of members of the Puritan clergy who were so effectively working together. Under their influence, Stone became increasingly committed to Puritan liturgical practices—so much so that he attracted the attention of Bishop Laud and in 1630 was silenced and deprived of his curacy.

Luckily for Stone and for Shepard, the term of Shepard's endowed lectureship at Earles Colne ran out the same year. Shepard's congregation raised the money to continue his position among themselves, and it was arranged according to the terms of endowment that the lecture-ship should be moved to fresh territory. Shepard managed to have it relocated to his home town of Towcester in Northamptonshire and to have it given to Stone, "knowing," he says of his family and friends in Towcester, "no greater love I could express to my poor friends than this" (50). Stone thereupon moved to Towcester with his wife, Rebecca, and one or two children. Two more children, Samuel and Sarah, were born and baptized there.

In the late spring of 1633, when Hooker returned to England, he went straight to Towcester to lay plans with his newly appointed assistant. At that time, an entertaining incident was reported which reveals something of what was known as Stone's "sudden and pleasant wit." Hooker was, of course, a much-wanted fugitive so that when he arrived on shore the church authorities lost no time in finding and following him. After his arrival at Stone's home in Towcester, as the two sat chatting and Hooker in a fatherly fashion was reproving his young colleague for "smoking of tobacco," a knock came at the door. Stone

> stepped unto the door, with his pipe in his mouth, and such an air
> of speech and look as gave him some credit with the officer. The
> officer demanded whether Mr. Hooker was not there? Mr. Stone
> replied with a braving sort of confidence, "What Hooker? Do
> you mean Hooker that lived once at Chelmsford?" The officer
> answered, "Yes, he!" Mr. Stone immediately... made this true
> answer, "If it be he you look for, I saw him about an hour ago,
> at such an house in the town, you had best hasten thither after
> him." The officer took this for a sufficient account and went his
> way. [14]

Stone clearly enjoyed defying and outwitting the authorities, a game in which Shepard would find the opportunity to participate before long.

The plans for emigration were soon completed. That summer, the Hookers with five children, the Stones with three, and John Cotton and his pregnant wife, Sarah, sailed along with two hundred other passengers on the ship *Griffen*, arriving in Boston on September 4, 1633. The Hookers and Stones went soon to their friends in Newtown, where on October 11 Winthrop records briefly: "a fast at Newtown, where Mr. Hooker was chosen pastor, and Mr. Stone teacher."[15] The first gathered church in Newtown was thus firmly established. When Thomas Shepard, then far off in the north of England, heard of the emigration and settlement of Cotton, Hooker, and Stone, he thought that he "saw the Lord departing from England" (57).

Thomas Shepard: "Tossed from the South to the North of England"

The story of Thomas Shepard's call to New England contains the same elements that we have seen in the story of Thomas Hooker and Samuel Stone: initial commitment to revival in the Church of England, stiffening resistance to the pressure for uniformity, and final loss of hope for the possibility of a creative ministry in England. Shepard, however, recorded the change of direction himself in a personal, step-by-step narrative. In his *Autobiography* he not only describes the harrowing experiences of confrontation, flight, and fear, but also gives a clear account of the transformation of one Puritan clergyman from a moderately critical priest of the Church of England, to a disaffected priest, to a pastor passionately committed to the creation of the gathered church. His story reveals as well a personality of far more warmth and complexity than appears in his hard-hitting, deep-cutting sermons of the English period.

At the time that Shepard accepted his first appointment as lecturer at the Church of St. Andrew in Earles Colne in 1627, his basic loyalty to the Church of England was unquestioned, although he believed that revival and reform were needed. Even some years later he was still able to speak of "our own church of England which is the most flourishing church in the world; never had church such preachers, such means."[16] This basic loyalty made it possible for Shepard in the early stages to adapt adroitly to the institutional requirements of the

Church of England without either taking serious issue with the authorities or compromising his own beliefs. Thus, he found it reasonable enough within the space of a few months in 1627 to accept the appointment to his lectureship through the good offices of Hooker's underground network of Puritan clergy; to be ordained to the priesthood by the Bishop of Peterborough; "to accept of the people's call" in Earles Colne in a distinctly congregational manner; and then finally, a few days later, in a swing back to episcopal authority, to procure from the Bishop of London a license to preach.

For a while he was able to preach quietly, gathering converts around himself. He describes how "the Lord had blessed [his] labors to diverse in and out of the town, especially to the chief house in the town, the Priory" (50). This was the manor house and home of the Harlakenden family, two of whom—Roger and his younger sister Mabel—would eventually come with Shepard to New England. With these people and others as a nucleus within the greater parish, Shepard's first flock was gathered. Its members were bound together in the Spirit, although not specifically covenanted, and so devoted to Shepard that when the three years of his lectureship had expired they "would not let [him] go," and collected money among themselves to support him. It was this lectureship that was then assumed by Samuel Stone and moved to Towcester.

Shepard's quiet did not last unbroken for long. In spite of his basic loyalty to the Church of England, he soon began to fall under suspicion—as Hooker and others had—simply because of the nature of his appointment, an endowed Puritan lectureship. His evangelical style of preaching and the fact that he insisted on preaching on forbidden subjects such as election and grace further undermined his security.[17] "Satan began to rage," he reports, "and the commissaries, registers and others began to pursue me" (50). He was cited by the local archdeacon's court in 1628 and 1629 and warned about the consequences of nonconformity.[18] Nevertheless, in spite of the pressure, he still did not describe himself as "a nonconformable man." Rather, he says, "for the most of that time I was not resolved either way, but was dark in those things" (50).

Then, on December 16, 1630, Shepard was called to appear before Bishop Laud in London and was deprived of his license to preach. His account brings to life the strong emotions on both sides of the Puritan question:

> *I was inhibited from preaching in the diocese of London by Dr. Laud, bishop of that diocese. As soon as I came in the morning about eight of the clock, falling into a fit of rage, he asked me what degree I had taken in the University. I answered him, I was a Master of Arts. He asked me of what College? I answered, of Emmanuel. He asked how long I had lived in his diocese. I answered, three years and upwards. He asked who maintained me all this while, charging me to deal plainly with him, adding withal that he had been more cheated and equivocated with by some of my malignant faction than ever was man by Jesuit, at the speaking of which words he looked as though blood would have gushed out of his face and did shake as if he had been haunted with an ague fit, to my apprehension by reason of his extreme malice and secret venom. I desired him to excuse me. He fell then to threaten me and withal to bitter railing. . . saying, You prating coxcomb! Do you think all the learning is in your brain? He pronounced his sentence thus: I charge you that you neither preach, read, marry, bury, or exercise any ministerial function in any part of my diocese, for if you do, and I hear of it, I will be upon your back and follow you wherever you go, in any part of the kingdom, and so everlastingly disenable you. . . . So away I went, and blessed be God that I may go to him.*[19]

Shaken, but still defiant, Shepard retired to the home of his friends and patrons, the Harlakenden family, under whose protection he continued to preach privately to his circle of local followers and converts. At the same time, in this sheltered environment he began to reflect about his church and to become gradually more disaffected from it. "The Lord let me see into the evil of the ceremonies, cross, surplice and kneeling," he wrote of this period (52).

Six months later, when Laud held a Bishop's Court at Kelvedon in Essex, he once again summoned Shepard and this time "charged [him] to depart the place" because he was "one who kept conventicles," or private worship services (52).[20]

It now became clear to Shepard that he must take his gospel to fresh ground, and he prepared to answer a call to serve as chaplain in the household of a Yorkshire gentleman in the town of Buttercrambe, not far from York. However, Bishop Laud had so raised his ire that he could not resist one last defiant provocation, wondering, "whether it was best to let such swine to root up God's plants in Essex and not to give him some check" (52). Accordingly, two days after the confrontation at Kelvedon, knowing that the Bishop was to preach at nearby Dunmow, Shepard and his friend, Thomas Weld, joined the congregation and made themselves known to Laud. Since Shepard had just been "charged to depart the place" and Laud had excommunicated Weld, this was boldly defiant behavior. In fury, Laud had Weld "committed to the pursuivant and bound over to answer [for] it at the High Commission," but Shepard and another friend who pulled him away "hastened our horses and away we rid as fast as we could and so the Lord delivered me out of the hand of that lion a third time" (53).

Shepard took a sorrowful farewell of his friends in Earles Colne and set off on horseback for Buttercrambe. After a difficult and sometimes frightening ride through rainstorms and flooded rivers, he arrived one night "very wet and late" at the great brick house of Sir Richard Darley, set back on a hill overlooking the village church at its foot (54).

Once again Shepard's preaching and compelling sincerity reached into the hearts of his listeners, this time not so much in the town and countryside as in a more intimate fashion within the large household of the Darley manor. One of his first converts was Margaret Touteville, a young relative of Sir Richard and woman-in-waiting to the lady of the house. Upon hearing Shepard preach a sermon at the marriage of the Darleys' daughter, "the Lord first touched the heart of Mistress Margaret." Like Hooker and Roger Williams in similar circumstances, Shepard fell in love and was soon married. He had for some time been looking for "a meet yoke fellow" (52). Having found her, he turned to his God in gratitude, promising "the Lord that this mercy should knit my heart the nearer to him" (55).

Although Shepard was gratified by the creation of a close fellowship among the inhabitants of the manor house at Buttercrambe, he struggled at the same time with the sense that his ministry was cramped with "none in the town or about it brought home [to God] (55)." And when Richard Neile, formerly Bishop of Winchester and an aggressive Laudian, was translated to the see of York, Shepard once again found himself in real danger. He, therefore, accepted the call that came from Northumberland, "far from any bishops," where he hoped that at last he "might preach . . . in peace" (56).

As we have seen, his ministry there stretched him to his utmost powers. With great urgency he struggled to convert the poor and uneducated in "this dark country" (57). At the same time, as the difficulties of his position became more untenable and especially when he was once again forced to go into hiding, he found himself driven further in his disaffection from the Church of England, just as he had been under similar circumstances in Essex. He came, he says of his ministry in and around Newcastle, "to read and know more of the ceremonies, church government and estate, and the unlawful standing of bishops than in any other place" (56). Most radical of all, he became "convinced not only of the evil of ceremonies but of mixed communion [communion shared with baptized but not necessarily converted Christians] and of joining with such in sacraments" (57).

At the same time that Shepard's congregational stance became more and more uncompromising, he began to experience his plight as an "exiled condition" and "to listen to a call to New England." He had heard that Cotton, Hooker, Stone and Weld were there. He had also received a letter from John Bridge, recently elected deacon of the new church in Newtown, who had known Shepard as well as Hooker in Essex. Bridge wrote "of providing a place for a company of us" (55, 57). In England there were other friends who urged him "to go to New England, there to live together" (57). The community that they had known together in England they hoped to form again in New England.

However, the call was not at first a clear one. No matter how frustrated he felt by being forced into "a disorderly manner of preaching privately" and no matter how much he began to long to exercise his "talent publicly," Shepard had great misgivings, knowing that he was needed in Northumberland. "It was true," he confessed, "that I should stay and suffer for Christ." He was also aware that his motives were not entirely disinterested. "My ends were mixed and I looked much to my own quiet," he wrote with a trace of shame. He weighed and listed the alternatives at length, and he talked to Margaret who "did long to see [him] settled there in peace" (58). Eventually, if reluctantly, a decision was made, and in June of 1634 Thomas and Margaret; their six-month-old son, Thomas, who had been born in Northumberland; and their maid boarded "a ship laden with coals" and sailed down the coast from Newcastle to Ipswich, the first leg of their journey to the New World (58).

Now began a harrowing period of pursuit, hiding, and enforced idleness for the Shepards while they waited for passage to New England. "Truly," Shepard wrote of this period, "I found this time of my life wherein I was so tossed up and down and had no place of settling, but kept secret . . . the most uncomfortable and fruitless time to my own soul especially that ever I had in my life" (59). To add to their anxiety, Margaret was pregnant again, and they feared that her lying in would lead to their discovery as well as to danger for the friends who sheltered them.

During the eighteen months before their final departure, they experienced near shipwreck as the ship in which they first set sail was driven northward by high winds from Harwich to Yarmouth and was nearly "swallowed up of the sands." They were saved miraculously when their dragging anchor finally took hold: "the cable was let out so far that a little rope held the cable, and the cable the little anchor, and the little anchor the great ship in this great storm" (62). The terror of the moment never completely left Shepard. From this time on, images of the menacing sea occur over and over in his sermons. In the chaotic days that followed, their baby son, Shepard's "first born child, very precious to my soul and dearly beloved of me" took ill. When he died, the loss was made even more acutely painful by the necessity for secrecy. Little Thomas "was buried at Yarmouth," says Shepard, and

"I durst not be present lest the pursuivants should apprehend me and I should be discovered, which was a great affliction and very bitter to me and my dear wife" (63).

After having "been tossed from the south to the north of England" and back, they at last set sail in the ship *Defense* on August 10, 1635, to begin the voyage to New England, bringing with them their four-month-old son, Thomas, named for the first. With them also was Shepard's half-brother, Samuel, and members and friends of the Harlakenden family, who had so generously sheltered Shepard at Earles Colne and had more recently come to join him and Margaret as they waited in Norfolk.

Shepard's ministry in England was a highly personal one. He had reached out to people to convert them. He had sheltered and nourished them in close communions pressed together by the hostile environment that surrounded them. And he had reached out, too, in personal need, seeking companionship for his own soul. Over and over in his *Autobiography* he speaks of what his friends meant to him, of how "the Harlakendens were so many fathers and mothers to me," of how "the Lord turned all the sons and Sir Richard . . . unto me" at Buttercrambe, of the "many sweet friends and Christian acquaintance" at Heddon-on-the-Wall, and of the "sweet fellowship one with another and also with God" that they enjoyed as they waited through the winter of 1634 to 1635 in Norfolk (52, 55, 56, 64).

Richard Harlakenden, the older brother of Roger and one of Shepard's close friends from this period, wrote with great feeling after he heard of Shepard's death many years later:

> The Lord made him to me a messenger, one of a thousand; even one of the most precious spiritual instruments and friends, that ever I have yet met withal, in my poor pilgrimage, and I am persuaded, the like he was to many others: for he was one that preached powerfully, lived holily, died comfortably.[21]

That many others did feel as Harlakenden felt was clearly demonstrated by the number of followers who made the journey to be with Shepard in New England. Among the members of the first church in

Newtown were men and women from Earles Colne, from Butter-crambe, from Newcastle and Heddon-on-the-Wall, and even some from his hiding place in Norfolk. These people can be traced from Shepard's own account and from passenger lists, but also through the confessions of faith that they made in Shepard's Cambridge church, where many of them recalled what he had meant to them in England. In New England we shall see more of this tender, pastoral Shepard as well as a somewhat less stern preacher as he adapted his message to a new role in new circumstances.

4

The Church of Christ at Cambridge, 1632–1649

The Church in Transition:
The Ministry of Thomas Hooker

In the absence of surviving church records or any sermons that can be accurately attributed to Hooker's years in Cambridge, we can only guess at the character of his pastorate there. The Braintree Company surely must have welcomed him joyfully, and Hooker must have continued to instruct his flock in the healing process that comes with God's grace, as he had in England and would do once again in Hartford. This much we may reasonably surmise. However, sources outside the immediate church community lead us to believe also that this two-and-a-half-year period was one characterized by restlessness and discontent for Hooker. For the newly gathered church, it was a period of transition, a prelude to its firm and lasting establishment under Shepard's leadership.

From the beginning, Newtown had been a community in flux. Originally settled in 1630 as the prospective capital of the Bay Colony, it had consistently failed to develop a stable population. After it proved rather quickly to be an unsuitable capital as well as a dwelling place uncongenial to the taste of the colony's governor, John Winthrop, it remained very sparsely settled until the advent of the Braintree Company in the summer of 1632. Then followed a brief period of determined settlement, during which houses were built; fields allotted, cleared, and planted; and the simple meeting house built, all in preparation for the anticipated coming of their pastor and teacher,

Thomas Hooker and Samuel Stone, in the autumn of 1633.

However, even the advent of Hooker and the influx of settlers that accompanied him did not provide stability in Newtown or in its first church. After only eight months, Hooker was ready to move on once again—this time into the wilderness of the Connecticut valley.[1] The reasons for his restlessness are obscure. Many explanations have been offered over many years both by his contemporaries and by a succession of scholars. Hooker's own explanation, expressed in the petition of his party to the General Court asking for permission for removal, was the "want of accommodation for their cattle, . . . the fruitfulness and commodiousness of Connecticut," and, "the strong bent of their spirits to move thither."[2] There may, indeed, have been some truth in the assertion that more pasture was needed for grazing since Cambridge was at that time a narrow strip of land sandwiched between Watertown and Charlestown. However, the promise of more land offered by Watertown and Boston did not lessen for long the determination of the Hooker party to depart. One irritated and hurt Massachusetts resident suggested that the reason for their rejection of the Bay Colony was their weakness, their want of the tenacious determination necessary to wrest a living from eastern Massachusetts soil: they "took dislike of every little matter; the plowable plains were too dry and sandy for them, and the rocky places demanded so much in toil of hand and hoe" that "they deemed it unsupportable."[3]

A more likely reason and one supported by some modern scholarship was suggested by another contemporary, who suspected that there was, "a great division of judgement in matters of religion among good ministers and people which moved Mr. Hooker to remove." Hooker and John Cotton were by far the most distinguished theologians as well as the most powerful preachers in the Bay Colony. Perhaps, observed a New England historian two generations later, "two such eminent stars . . . could not well continue in one and the same orb."[4] Whether or not they were rivals, the increasing divergence in their views was becoming more and more obvious in the rising tension that preceded the Antinomian Controversy. Hooker, like Shepard later, could not accept the high Calvinism of Cotton that allowed for no preparatory motion toward grace by the sinner. Nor could he accept the tendency toward antinomianism that Cotton's preaching inspired. It was even rumored that he had come to distrust the requirement of a public "relation" for church membership and that "before he went away [he] preached against it." Rather than flirting on the edge of what he perceived as dangerously Spirit-centered emotionalism, Hooker held to the more orderly psychology of preparation in which his ministry had always been grounded.[5]

A final component in Hooker's motivation may have been his primary commitment to his calling as a pastor and healer of souls, which was being compromised by his incessant involvement in public affairs.[6] His prominence as a theologian and Puritan activist had meant that in the near-theocracy of the Bay Colony he had been drawn into local politics as an advisor almost from the moment he set foot in Boston. The magistrates called upon him to consult with them in state controversies, both great and small, from the pros and cons of the participation of Newtown in building a fort in Boston to the weighty affair of the trial of Roger Williams. All this activity and responsibility was time-consuming and in some cases emotionally exhausting. How uncongenial and frustrating Hooker actually found the involvement we cannot know for sure, but it is clear that after his removal to Connecticut the production of published sermons, pamphlets, and books resumed.[7]

The exodus from Newtown to Hartford began in the spring and summer of 1635. So many of Hooker's congregation had gone on before him that when Shepard and his party arrived in October they, "found many houses empty and many persons willing to sell" (66). During the course of the winter of 1635 to 1636 the two congregations overlapped in the meeting house. Hooker, as pastor, baptized young Thomas Shepard there, and then on February 1, 1636, Shepard's church was gathered. Although conscious of being in some sense two churches, the two congregations must have continued to worship together through the winter and spring. In June, Hooker, with his wife and children and most of the remaining members of his congregation, departed for Hartford, thereby accomplishing a nearly complete transfusion in the first church in Cambridge. In the end, more than fifty families went with their pastor and teacher, taking their covenant and their church bell with them. The members of Shepard's congregation made the meetinghouse their own. In the context of congregational polity and in the eyes of the participants, a new church had been gathered with a new covenant. The sense among them of being a newly constituted holy community is suggested by the presence of three former members of Hooker's church among the candidates for admission to Shepard's church. These members were not simply absorbed in the change. Rather, they took part in the public rite of confession, and their "relations" were duly recorded by Shepard along with those of the new residents of Cambridge. However, in the wider context of the Church of Christ, the first church in Cambridge remained one church, transfused with new blood and a fresh commitment.[8]

Including the three whose conversion narratives were recorded by Shepard, there were ten families from the original congregation who remained in Cambridge concretely linking the new church to the old one. The person of John Bridge, one of its founders and consistently one of its leaders, provided special continuity for the community and for Shepard, who had come to Newtown partly at his urging. Bridge, a widower at fifty-three with two sons, had joined the Braintree Company to begin a new life with the Puritan venture in New England in response to the Essex ministry of both Hooker and Shepard. As deacon in the Cambridge church for twenty-two years, as selectman for twelve, and deputy to the General Court for four, he served both church and community. For Shepard, the support his friend provided, together with the presence of the other families who had elected to remain with his congregation, must have given him confidence as he assumed the awful responsibility and welcome challenge of ministering to his newly gathered church.

The Church Established:
The Ministry of Thomas Shepard

"Time," said Thomas Shepard, "is a jewel of inestimable worth, a golden stream, dissolving and, as it were, continually running down by us out of one eternity into another, yet seldom taken notice of until it is quite passed away from us."[9] The continuity that Shepard speaks of in these words can be found beginning to emerge during the years of his pastorate with a concreteness that cannot be captured for the Hooker years. The survival of more complete church records from the period as well as a large collection of Shepard's sermons and personal papers make it possible to fill out a picture of the communal life in some detail. Beginning with Shepard's ministry, we can trace with some precision a gathered community in Cambridge that persists to the present day, renewed and regathered over the years as each new member joins the church.[10]

Basic to the evolution of Shepard's ministry was the radical change in role that he and his colleagues assumed as they adapted to new circumstances in New England. In England they had been a community united in their commitment to transform the Church of England. By bringing spiritual rebirth to countless individuals in their care, they had hoped in the end to revive an entire church. Their lives had been intense and focused, their purpose clear as they preached to convert, and as they sheltered from persecution the believers they had gathered around themselves. In New England, however, their mission was different. In their new country they were called to create a society of saints out of a wide ministry to every person in every town. In order to achieve their objective, they needed to establish an orderly commonwealth, led by those who were already saints, so that the gospel could flourish among the others. These new and unaccustomed responsibilities gradually effected the transformation of these radical English dissidents into the conservative architects of an established church in New England. In the process, they often watched in dismay as the Spirit they had felt to be so close seemed to be slipping away. In England it had been easy to kindle the fires of faith in secret conventicles. In New England it became much more difficult to keep those fires going.

These new perceptions and attitudes emerged slowly. When Thomas and Margaret Shepard arrived in New England, they felt only gratitude and thanksgiving, "rejoicing in our God," as Shepard wrote of their arrival in Boston. Margaret, almost certainly apprehensive about the worsening illness that would soon take her life, felt her "great desire now fulfilled, which was to leave me in safety from the hand of my enemies and among God's people, and also the child under God's precious ordinances" (66). Thomas, now free to use his powers to the fullest, began at once to devote himself to bringing into being in New England his vision of a "pure, chaste, virgin church."[11]

The essentials of Shepard's vision of the gathered church he held in common with all of his colleagues in New England. However, he shaped it in a manner that was distinctively his own. His ministry in Cambridge can be divided into three overlapping phases in which his ideal of the pure church was refined. He first participated in its creation. Then, as it became threatened from both inside and out, he began to defend it fiercely. Finally, in a more peaceful period, he devoted himself to the nurture of the holy community, defining it more clearly, teaching its members how to participate in it with all their hearts, and pondering how best to preserve its pure form for posterity. The message that he preached to his flock in these three periods turned gradually away from evangelism toward a focus on deepening the spirituality of his flock and elucidating for its members matters of practical doctrine, such as the observation of the Sabbath and the church membership of children.

Immediately after his arrival, Shepard set himself to the primary task of building his church. He embarked at once on a series of sermons designed both to awaken his people spiritually and to prepare them for church membership. He would, he said, "woo them for Christ," an approach he believed to be the "main work of the ministry."[12] Since from his own experience he knew that faith comes only when "the affections are wrought upon," he used language intended to touch hearts and arouse spiritual longing, speaking sometimes with gentleness, sometimes with a passion that evoked tender, often erotic overtones, as in the following passage:

> This day thou shalt no sooner set thy heart on Christ but he falls in love with thee, and will take thee with joy; thou thinkest he will be angry if thou closest with him and love him; no, it will be

the joy of heaven, of Jesus Christ himself.... He will exceed-
ingly comfort thee.... Once love him and he will never loose
thee. No sin shall part thee and him... the covenant is everlast-
ing and so undertaken for by the Lord that it can never be
broken. [13]

To prepare his congregation for church membership, Shepard in-
structed them in the generally accepted steps according to which a
genuine conversion experience must proceed. Although, in broad out-
line, his teaching about the stages of conversion followed the classical
ordo salutis, in several matters of emphasis it was quite different. He
believed that the whole scheme was more crucially important than did
many of his colleagues. For him there was nothing theoretical about
the order of salvation. It was part of the structure of reality, like the
ground beneath his feet; and the steps that it comprised he called
"God's rule."[14] There was, according to Shepard, a perfect correspondence between God's motions of grace and the anatomy of the human
soul that made it imperative for the soul in search of salvation to know
what to expect. For, although one could not by one's performance influence God's preordained purpose, an understanding of what he was
about made it possible at least to recognize his voice and to respond
when he called. Shepard believed it to be a primary pastoral responsibility to provide the teaching that would keep his people alert and
aware that grace was always near. If his teaching about the perils of the
journey to salvation was harsh, it was because he believed that as a
careful pastor he must prepare his people for a harsh reality.

In addition to his firm insistence on the need to understand the order of salvation, one aspect of Shepard's teaching on the subject is distinctive. He was, more than any of his colleagues, concerned with the
need for the soul to be humbled before the law and with the psychology of that process. Based on his own conversion experience, he took
an extreme position, insisting that before faith could come in, the soul
must surrender to God in humiliation so complete that if it were God's
will, even damnation could be accepted. Of his own conversion, as we
have seen above, he says that at last he was able "to leave myself with

him to do with me what he would, and then and never until then I found rest . . . and the terrors of the Lord began to assuage sweetly" (46). Perhaps in order to make the approach to such a position more accessible conceptually, and again in accordance with his own experience, Shepard inserted a fourth step in the classical three-part scheme of conviction, humiliation, and justification. The penitent believer, according to Shepard, would experience after conviction of sin (which had been defined as primarily a matter of intellectual recognition), another identifiable state of mind that he called "compunction." This was an emotional apprehension of the plight in which the soul found itself, "a pricking of the heart, or wounding of the soul with such fear and sorrow for sin and misery as severs the soul from sin."[15] Then would come the complete surrender of humiliation, and then faith.

When new believers felt ready for membership in Shepard's Cambridge church, the process of admission was conducted in accordance with the new criterion peculiar to New England congregationalism, requiring them "to declare what work of grace the Lord had wrought in them."[16] Although the requirement had been worked out shortly before Shepard's arrival, he welcomed it personally, both as a vital expression of his own ideal for the church and as a tool that could be used in its creation. He affirmed a practice that would surely aid in the creation of a pure church by identifying those "visible saints" who had been touched by the Spirit through the revealing process of public confession. Equally important, he believed in the enormous value of these oral "relations" to deepen the life of the community and increase its Spirit-centeredness. Public confession moved people, Shepard said, "for the increase of their own joy to see God glorified and Christ's name professed, and his virtues held forth, and for the increase of their love to those that join them."[17]

Accordingly, when receiving new members, Shepard was attentive and deeply serious. An indication of the scrutiny he gave to the confessions of candidates for membership was his refusal, at a meeting of clergy and magistrates in the spring of 1636, to assent to the gathering of a new church in Dorchester. By way of explaining his attitude, he wrote to Richard Mather, the pastor, that he "was not satisfied scarce in any measure with their profession of faith," and further cautioned Mather "to be very wary and very sharp in looking to the hearts and spirits" of those who would join his church.[18] For his own congregation, he kept careful notebooks in which he recorded the narratives presented by prospective candidates for admission, again indicating the importance he attached to the process and the attention with which he listened to each individual story. Two of these notebooks survive, one for the years 1638 to 1645 and a second, smaller collection for the years 1648 to 1649.[19]

Shepard's apparent sternness in scrutinizing the fitness of prospective members was not inflexible. He had no illusions about the fallibility of the screening process. "There will," he said, "be tares and wheat, there will be chaff and corn, there will be wise and foolish virgins, there will be good and bad mingled together in the churches until the world's end."[20] Shepard thus never identified his church of "visible saints" who testified to an experience of grace with God's true invisible church of all the elect, living and dead and as yet unborn. His aim was not to create a church of the elect, although Puritans have very often been accused of that, but to build a church that would show forth the Spirit. "We profess," Shepard said, ". . . that it is not real, but visible faith . . . that constitutes a visible church, which faith so professed is called visible not in the judgement of certainty, . . . but in the judgement of charity which hopes the best."[21]

In actual practice in his own church, Shepard does seem to have judged in charity. He was interested in repentance and true sincerity rather than in any details of content the confessor might reveal. Distrustful of histrionics and excess of emotion as possibly insincere as well as disruptive of the congregation, he also feared the potential for antinomian enthusiasm that might lodge in unrestrained self-expression. He preached against the "many odd confessions by those that are received and extravagant, enlarged discourses." There was, he insisted, no "necessity of tears, or violent and tumultuous complaints; the deepest sorrows run with least noise." He urged rather as modes of expression simplicity, directness, and sincerity, "such as may be of special use unto the people of God, such things as tend to show, thus was I humbled, then thus was I called, then thus have I walked, though with many weaknesses since;... and thus the Lord hath delivered me."[22]

Judging from the accounts that Shepard recorded, he was a compassionate and flexible listener. The confessions range in content from some that are fragmentary and clearly uttered under stress to elaborate statements of the classical *ordo salutis* by Nathaniel Eaton and Henry Dunster, two clerical members of the congregation and accomplished public speakers. All were received and recorded with care: men and women, masters and servants, illiterate and highly educated alike. There is no evidence in the earlier collection that any penitent was turned away. Shepard's record is, however, one of "diverse propounded to be received and were *entertained* as members."[23] Possibly there were others, unrecorded, who were not "entertained as members" in order to insure the purity of the church. In the later collection one candidate, Abraham Arrington (Errington), was apparently denied admission since his name appears much later as having been accepted into membership in 1663. There is, however, no indication in his narrative of his having been unsuccessful when he first applied in 1648.[24]

As the holy community of which he had dreamed began to become a reality, Shepard rejoiced, but not for long. No sooner was it a palpable creation than he felt it threatened from within and from without. The inward threat came from a cooling of spiritual ardor, caused, he believed, by "the temptation of this place."[25] Its peace, its hardship for some, and its prosperity for others had made many people feel less urgent about the state of their souls. Shepard addressed the situation: "Take heed that you grow not secure. You have the pillow of peace to lie on, and the cares of the world to make you dream away your time, and you have no pinching persecutions to awaken you." "Have you forgot your God," he said on another occasion, "and forgot... the business for which you made this great undertaking?... Hath not the Lord, by a stretched out arm, brought thee and thine through seas and dangers and delivered you wonderfully? Are not... all your promises forgotten?... Look upon men in the fields and conversings and buy-ings and sellings; where is the daily, weekly watchfulness over our thoughts and tongues?... Are not men's ears sealed up?... O, how many men are there that become quite sermon-proof nowadays!"[26]

A more specific and far more immediately threatening menace to Shepard's fragile new church was the antinomian heresy of Anne Hutchinson and her followers. Long before the perception had become general among the clergy and magistrates of Massachusetts Bay that the law of God and the very stability of society were severely threatened by these "gospel wantons," as Shepard would soon call them, he became troubled.[27] Part of his fear probably lay in his lingering memory of the antinomian temptation that he had experienced at the time of his conversion.[28] Although he had not succumbed to the lure of "that glorious estate of perfection" (44) as a youth and would not in the future, the disavowed but persistent longing for perfect assurance may have added emotional impact to his doctrinal stance against antinomianism, contributing to an attitude that became nearly an obsession.

As early as the spring of 1636, when he had only been in Cambridge for four or five months, he sensed danger. The preaching of John Cotton made him uneasy, and so "for the farther clearing up of the truth," Shepard wrote to him expressing his disquiet. He feared Cotton's insistence on the impotence of the sinner, who must wait passively for the coming of the Spirit, and he distrusted Cotton's refusal to allow the searching penitent to find evidence of grace in a sanctified life. Drawing from his own experience with the "superlative raptures" of antinomian sects in England, he concluded the letter with a warning against those who might "do your people and ministry hurt, before you know it."[29] Shepard sounded these warnings throughout the rest of his ministry, with vehemence during the crisis but also with echoes of fear for all of his days.

He was deeply involved in the crisis at every stage from its beginnings in religious revival and theological controversy to its resolution in the excommunication and banishment of Anne Hutchinson. Shepard's stance was unwavering even as he tried to help her, visiting her frequently and counseling her when she was confined in the home of Joseph Weld in Roxbury to await her heresy trial in the Boston church. In the end, when he used the information she had confided to him as evidence against her in the trial, he had no doubt as to the rightness and necessity of so doing, as we have seen. The danger to the churches and the commonwealth was extreme, he believed, and he was determined through any means necessary to rout the heretic and to keep his town of Cambridge "spotless from the contagion of the opinions" (70). This he succeeded in doing, largely by dint of his incessant preaching on the subject, especially in a series of sermons preached at his Thursday lectures during this period. He warned at the outset against division in the newly created, fragile church:

> Love the truth, receive no opinion differing from the most approved in the church; but weep, and pray, and ask counsel, and tremble to entertain a thought of contention. . . . O, keep the peace of the church and rend it not. . . . Love one another sincerely, and you cannot but live together quietly. [30]

Shepard believed the antinomian doctrine to be seductive and easy as well as superficial and its perpetrators arrogant: "They close with Christ to make them[selves] happy, not to make them holy; but they thus closing with him, think they have him, and hence have some kind of communion with him and hence think they are espoused to him, and more familiar with him than others." [31]

Shepard countered the apparent chaos of direct revelation with strong adherence to a powerful and ambiguous faith that was consistent with his rejection of antinomianism but reached far beyond it. He preached both grace and the "use of the law" as a "rule of life unto a Christian." He proclaimed an almighty God, and at the same time gave hope to humbled men and women that, with openness to the Spirit, they might participate in their own pilgrimage of faith through following "God's rule" of preparation for salvation. Although he increasingly preached about the reality of assurance, he was always watchful for lapses into doubt and sin. [32]

The final phase of Shepard's ministry filled the years from about

1640 until his death in 1649. This was a far more tranquil time than he had ever experienced in his ministry in England or New England, and he was able during these years to realize his hopes for the Cambridge church more fully, in a manner both conservative and creative. It was a period at once of retrenchment and of flowering. Added to the urgent need to restore order in the churches in the aftermath of the Antinomian Controversy was a new source of anxiety for the clergy. Increasingly, they became apprehensive about the danger of English Parliamentary interference in the New England Congregational Way. However right they believed it to be, they knew very well that from the perspective of the mother country it was manifestly illegal, especially in its exclusiveness. These fears led Shepard, along with many of his colleagues, to hasten to define the nature of their church clearly so that it could be both protected in the present and preserved for posterity. To this end, he participated in the synod that met in Cambridge to produce the Cambridge Platform of Church Discipline of 1648, a document expressive of its time in its insistence on the New England Way as the only divine way, but that also laid the permanent foundation of modern congregationalism. The document, for example, sets forth the balance between the independence and interdependence of individual churches and defines the character of a ministry elected and called by the people.[33]

For Shepard personally, these were creative years, in which he devoted himself to nurturing the spiritual lives of his parishioners and to building the Christian community in which those lives were rooted. At this juncture in his ministry, he turned from his instruction of new members in God's plan for their conversion and sanctification to fresh ground. Although he never left off his warnings against antinomians and other spiritual radicals or entirely abandoned the use of "terror to the wicked," Shepard began to preach more in a vein that would provide "a ground of comfort" to God's people, deepening and stabilizing their faith.[34] For the anxious and as yet unconverted, he spoke in biblical language of the small beginnings of faith for many people, which must be grasped and held and acted upon:

Know this kingdom of God is at first like a grain of mustard seed,
some little lying under the will of Christ; if it be in truth, blessed
be God for it; the kingdom of God is come, and the soul doth
weep and mourn after the Lord, that the Lord would bring every
thought into subjection.[35]

Of much larger moment in this period is Shepard's counsel to the
faithful who, though converted, continued to lapse into sin and
doubt. He reassured them by placing their dilemma in the larger context of God's plan for redemption. Union with God was never absolute. Sin would linger, but for God's faithful people reunion would
come—along with growth in faith and renewed commitment:

When have the faithful sweeter naps in Christ's bosom than after
sorest troubles, longest eclipses of God's pleased face? When do
their souls cleave closer to the Lord than when they are ready to
forsake the Lord, and the Lord them? Certainly fire is wholly
carried upward, when that which suppresseth it makes it at last
break out into greater flame. Peter falls from Christ; yet . . . his
fall being greater, his faith clave the closer to the Lord Christ for-
ever after it.[36]

Shepard knew whereof he spoke. His journal is shot through with
his continuing struggles with doubt and falling away from God; but,
over and over again, through self examination, repentance, and meditation on the promises of Christ, he would find reunion and a measure
of assurance in the process.[37] As he had earlier called the members of
his congregation to conversion out of his own experience, so later he
counseled them from his own experience of the cycle of reconversion.
The key to reunion for the faithful is to focus on the promise, even
when life seems darkest:

When we can see no good come by affliction, but find ourselves
more dead and dull, and also God to frown upon us, and yet we
trust in God, and believe the promise, and stay our souls upon

God's word: this is to live by faith as we are commanded. . . .
Here is comfort against all [our] sins, God hath promised to do
them away. . . . Therefore, . . . hold up thy head and take com-
fort to thyself.

The faithful should not, however, expect instant relief from God but,
"wait humbly under our present condition; until God grant our desire,
God's time is the best time."[38]

Consistent with Shepard's emphasis on deepening the spiritual life
of his congregation in this period was a renewed focus on the nurture
of his holy community. This "concern for the communal aspect of
Christian experience," in the estimation of one scholar, lay at the
heart of Puritanism, and it was a central aspect of Shepard's ministry
from the beginning.[39] From his English days in secret conventicles,
through the early exhilaration of gathering and settling a new church
in New England, and through his supreme endeavor to keep his congregation "spotless from the contagion of the opinions," Shepard
prized the warmth and dynamism of the holy community he was building. In the last years of his ministry, having the peace and leisure to
teach his flock more about their participation in communal life must
have given him deep satisfaction.

As in the confessional requirement for church membership, the inspiration for the ideal of Christian community came from the Apostle
Paul, the guiding spirit of Puritans. For Shepard, the dynamic, grow-
ing character of the body of Christ, "building itself up in love" (Eph.
4:16), provided the criterion for judging and shaping the elements of
the community. "Members are not to stand like beautiful pictures in
church windows," he said, "but they are to be living stones in God's
building, not only to build up themselves, but one another also."[40]

Shepard trained his congregation in every aspect of the sacred obligation of church membership. The responsibility for the admission of
new members was primary since it established the original direct link
with the Spirit: "Be very careful in receiving in of members into
churches. One ill man will be a spot and pollution to all the rest . . .
therefore try them well."[41]

The exercise of discipline within the congregation was a logical consequence of the attempt to create a pure, Spirit-centered church. Discipline would keep its members pure and knit together in love. Members were to watch one another and report wrongdoing, from swearing and drunkenness to adultery and theft. Watchfulness was to be practiced, however, with balanced wisdom and with love. Shepard advised his flock thus:

> Be not a man of shallow head who censures and condemns all that do not magnify him and reverence the dust of his feet. And yet it is another sinful extreme to swallow down all the flies that be in the cup, and to think too charitably of every one that does profess. [42]

Members were to support one another in the faith in and out of church: "Let every man get up and fall to this work of mutual exhorting; go and visit one another, go and speak often to one another." There are several ways to reach church members, he said: "Labor to know the state of thy brethren . . . what their sleepy neglects be, and sins are. . . . Speak a word to awaken him, for which Christ shed his blood."

If one parishioner was unacquainted with another, Shepard suggested:

> inquire, with a spirit of much love, how it is with them. . . . How have you found your heart since last sermon, Sabbath, fast, affliction? . . . Relate thy own condition; this is a most lovely provocation and exhortation. . . . Speak oft to one another, forsake not your assembling, visit one another, pray for one another. [43]

Shepard warns against division in his close community, against those who may "sit by the fireside, and censure, and whisper, and make offenses, and take offenses; and minds divide, and hearts divide." Instead, they are to walk together in "a spirit of dear Christ-like love one to another, every one to all." It is a love that means, "comforting those that be sad," for "there are many sad hearts in God's church, and sad things are as wounds to a man's limbs, that make him halt or fall." And it is a love that requires prayer, "earnest prayer for the church, and all in it besides thyself," for "it is one of the greatest privileges that a man hath, when once he hath a share in all the prayers of the saints as his own."[44]

Through this kind of preaching and through a tireless personal ministry, Shepard built a community that strengthened and comforted people for whom the church was almost the only emotional resource and moral guide. Having been recently uprooted and torn from the long security of tradition, they had been planted in an unfamiliar and lonely wilderness where there were not yet any firm guidelines to shape their way of life. Shepard counseled them and he taught them to bear one another's burdens, to forgive, to acknowledge their dependence on God, and to find strength through faith in Jesus Christ.

Shepard's community took good care of its own, but it was not an accepting place for strangers or a place that could tolerate the slightest theological deviation. His church became, in fact, increasingly exclusive as the town grew larger and a smaller and smaller proportion of the people could testify to an experience of grace. It must also have been oppressive for some, as busybodies pried moralistically into each other's lives. Shepard fought the pettiness of such people, but he did foster exclusiveness. He believed in it with his whole heart as the only way to protect the pure church. "To open the door for all comers into the church" was, he said, "open whoredom, too gross, too shameful."[45]

The record of what his contemporaries had to say about Shepard brings out a dimension of his personality unrevealed by his sermons. Responses have survived from many different quarters. There are reactions from casual observers drawn to him by his preaching. There is the more serious scrutiny of some of his colleagues, and there is the exceedingly complex response of the sixty-seven of his parishioners whose confessions of faith he recorded. Several consistent themes emerge from this varied collection.

Even allowing for the extravagant rhetoric of a generation that made it an article of faith to revere its founding fathers, Shepard does seem to have been an effective preacher. It was said that people would travel on foot thirty miles from Ipswich to hear him preach those quiet but carefully crafted sermons that would "heal as well as sting." Edward Johnson, a lay contemporary, could not find enough superlatives to praise him in "whose soul the Lord shed abroad his love so abundantly, that thousand of souls have cause to bless God for him."[46]

Some people may have come to hear him preach of love, as he often did, especially toward the end of his ministry, melting hearts as well as breaking them. However, he was most famous for his formidable preaching of the law and the necessity of achieving humiliation before receiving faith. From his own scrupulous self-scrutiny, he knew all of the doubts and dodges of the human heart. And he forced his hearers to examine themselves with the same honesty, frightening them with dire consequences if they were lazy or dishonest in their self-confrontation.

Some, like Shepard's successor Jonathan Mitchel, blessed him for his severity. Shepard's preaching, he said, "terrified" him and yet, looking back at his student days under Shepard's guidance, he said, "I know not how I could have more cause to bless God with wonder than for those four years."[47]

There were others who criticized Shepard for erecting a stumbling block to faith by his inflexible and harsh insistence on preparatory contrition, compunction, and humiliation. In declaring, "what was required to make a Sound Believer," said the Reverend Giles Fermin, Shepard had "made such requisites, as trouble many, and cut off most of the sound, with the unsound Christians." Shepard remained adamant, insisting that,

> the gospel consolations and grace which some would have dished out as the dainties of the times . . . may possibly tickle and ravish some . . . but if axes and wedges withal be not used to hew and break this rough, unhewn, bold . . . age, I am confident the work . . . of all these men's ministry will be at best but mere hypocrisy.[48]

A perusal of the confessions of Shepard's parishioners makes one wonder if there may have been some truth in Fermin's criticism. They are not what the rhetoric of the Commonwealth's founders might have led us to believe New England confessions would be—perhaps hymns of grateful praise to God for deliverance from persecution or triumphant stories of salvation in the wilderness. They are not like that at all. They speak much more of the enormous hardship of life in the Bay Colony, of loneliness and disappointment, and of anxiety brought on by the demands of their difficult faith than they do of the joy of Christian commitment. Only a handful speak with firm confidence of God's love, but without exception, they all speak of the search for humiliation.

Such an apparent gap between the vision and the reality of life experienced in New England should be approached with some caution in view of the importance of the cycle of conversion and reconversion in the Puritan ethos.[49] A story of triumphant assurance and the removal of all anxiety would have been suspect, presumptuous, even antinomian. There is, nonetheless, a genuine perception of a dream unrealized that is rooted in the tangled web of hopes and fears, of social and religious pressures, and of exile and alienation in which these people found themselves. A recent student of the confessions has suggested that for them the voyage to New England had almost become one with the pilgrimage to salvation. When they found "people living otherwise than I looked for," and "meeting with sorrows," as one of them said, many of them were filled with an unexpected disappointment that choked them with guilt and fear. They could not blame God, but neither could they recapture the faith that had brought them to New England. Cornered and in despair, they blamed themselves and mourned for their loss of faith and "deadness" of heart.[50]

A second explanation may be more directly related to the preaching and personality of Shepard. The severe demands of his view of preparation for salvation increased their sense of guilt and widened the breach between them and their God, leaving the more insecure of them cowering in fear. And yet, in spite of what appears to have been at times an almost merciless pressure that Shepard placed on them, they did not fault him for it. They simply felt, as he did, that he was telling them the painful truth—a truth from which he himself did not flinch. He was doing his utmost to help them to find their way to grace, and they were grateful. They loved him for the infinite pains he took with them, and they knew that he loved them.

The impact of Shepard's preaching and personality on the Cambridge community and beyond was deep. When, in November of 1637, the General Court made the decision "to take order for a college," the location of the new institution that would become Harvard College was decided upon partly because of the presence in Cambridge of Shepard's "orthodox and soul-flourishing ministry."[51] The influence of both his conservatism and the acuteness of his observations about the workings of the human heart persisted in the intellectual mainstream of the colonies for at least one hundred years. His conservatism helped to stabilize the church, although perhaps at some cost to its creativity. His theology of conversion reverberated through the eighteenth century, appearing especially in the work of Jonathan Edwards.[52] After that, the thread becomes more difficult to trace, although new editions of his sermons continued to be issued well into the nineteenth century.

The Shepard legacy has had a rather specific impact on the spiritual heritage and even the fortunes of the Congregational branch of the two churches that emerged from the controversy over unitarian doctrine in the early nineteenth century. When, in 1829, the Church of Christ at Cambridge divided to become the churches now known as the First Church in Cambridge, Congregational, United Church of Christ, and the First Church in Cambridge, Unitarian Universalist, the Congregationalists very consciously associated themselves with their orthodox, trinitarian roots in Shepard's church. In so doing, they began an affirmation that persisted into the pastorate of Alexander McKenzie (1867–1912) and, although in a much less specific sense, even to the present day. McKenzie's emotional description of the scene on the day that Abiel Holmes, pastor of the church at the time of its division, was forced to withdraw from his pulpit at the

Cambridge meetinghouse finds him "crossing the street, as the founder of the church had crossed the sea" to begin "Divine service in the old Court House."[53] The new church established by Holmes and his congregation was called, at his suggestion, The First Church in Cambridge and Shepard Congregational Society; and the present meetinghouse, built in the same tradition, was known until well into the twentieth century as the Shepard Memorial Church. Holmes's successor, Nehemiah Adams, continued to foster interest in the Shepard heritage and in 1832 edited the first printing of Shepard's *Autobiography*, the proceeds of which were used to purchase communion silver for the new church. The next pastor, John A. Albro, was a serious student of Shepard as well as an ardent admirer. He wrote the first full-length biography, *The Life of Thomas Shepard* (1842).[54] His successor, McKenzie, devoted four of his eight *Lectures on the History of the First Church in Cambridge* (1873) to Shepard.

In the city of Cambridge, too, there are reminders of Shepard's presence. Two memorial plaques point to his role in the early history of the town. One was recently erected on the Dawes Triangle near the Cambridge Common. It describes the importance of the seventeenth-century church heritage for the town and for the contemporary Harvard Square churches that are descended from it. Another plaque on the edge of Harvard Yard indicates the spot where Shepard's house stood and where he meditated in his garden every day, living out the life Cotton Mather described as his "trembling walk with God."[55]

The Role of Women in the Village Church

Cambridge women left little evidence of their presence in the early years of the Church of Christ in Cambridge. However, it is possible to discover some clear indications of their role in the congregation, especially if their story is approached from more than one perspective. An examination of the social and religious context in which they lived can provide a background for the understanding of two contemporary sources that offer a more vivid glimpse of their specific circumstances. The sermons and memoirs of their pastor are relevant because Shepard's influence over the lives of his parishioners was enormous, and therefore, his expressed attitudes about women would have shaped their role and their self-image. In addition, the "relations" of thirty-one women among the sixty-seven confessions he recorded are a unique source, providing direct insight into their thoughts, emotions, and spirituality.

THE CONTEXT

The seventeenth-century perception of the nature and role of women was rooted in the long sweep of western culture and sanctioned by a literal understanding of the Bible. As a being made from man rather than from God in his "own image" (Gen. 1: 26) as man had been, and as "the weaker sex" of the first letter of Peter (1 Pet. 3:7), woman's nature was widely held to be physically, intellectually, and morally inferior to man's. Richard Baxter, an English Puritan divine of the second half of the seventeenth century, expressed the contemporary attitude:

> Except it be a very few that are patient and man-like, women are commonly of potent fantasies, and tender, passionate, impatient spirits, easily cast into anger, or jealousy or discontent: and of weak understandings, and therefore unable to reform themselves. They are betwixt a man and a child. [56]

Baxter's view of women was one of the underlying elements in the culture that determined and continuously shaped their role in society. Another element was the deeply felt need for the order provided by a hierarchical social structure. Even the late seventeenth-century feminist, Mary Astell, who championed the equality of the sexes, maintained in reference to the location of authority in the family, "There can be [no] society great or little, from empires down to private families, without a last resort, to determine the affairs of society by an irresistible sentence. . . . This supremacy must be fixed somewhere." [57]

Consistent with the perception of their weakness and with the needs of an orderly society, the position of women—maintained by all of the authority of church and state—was one of dependence and obedience to husbands and fathers: "by the law of God, of nature, of reason and by the Common Law, the will of the wife is subject to the will of the husband."[58] Their marriages were arranged by their parents, at which time their names and their property were merged in the names and property of their male protectors. It was a tradition embedded in Tudor society and expressed in law by the concept of *"femme covert"*:

> When a small brook or little river encorporateth with the Humber or Thames, the poor little rivulet loseth her name, it is carried and recarried with the new associate; it beareth no sway, it possesseth nothing during coverture. A woman as soon as she is married, is called "covert". . . . as it were, clouded and overshadowed; she hath lost her stream. . . . Her new self is her superior; her companion, her master.[59]

Not only could seventeenth-century women own no property, but they could neither make a contract nor write a will. They were excluded from the universities and from all of the halls of power in church and state. From our perspective, it is hard to imagine that, with such a formidable array of legal and social restraints binding their freedom and restricting their growth, they had any room left to find integrity as people. However, although all of the limitations that surrounded women were indeed real, these limitations did not go unchallenged, nor did they always prevail in the actual situations of daily life.

There was, in fact, something of a public debate on the position of women. One Agrippa von Nettesheim, an early sixteenth-century German writer and physician, frequently translated in the seventeenth century and quoted in the debate, went so far as to assert that "the true distinction of the sexes, consists merely in the different site of those parts of the body, wherein generation necessarily requires a diversity."[60] A personal and perhaps more deeply felt reproach was voiced in the seventeenth century by Anne Bradstreet, poet of Ipswich in the Bay Colony:

> I am obnoxious to each carping tongue
> Who says my hand a needle better fits,
> A poet's pen all scorn I should thus wrong,

For such despite they cast on female wits:
If what I do prove well, it won't advance
They'll say it's stol'n, or else it was by chance.[61]

The quiet realities of daily life—like the public debate and the publication and popularity of female authors such as Bradstreet, Katherine Philips, and later in the century, Aphra Behn—reveal a social situation for women that was not one of unambiguous subjugation.[62] There were loopholes in patriarchal authority and gaps between theory and practice that appeared in the demands of specific situations, especially in domestic situations. Together with differences in personality, which always bring flexibility to human relations, these variables gave many women some private authority and even some opportunity for personal development. For example, the responsibility associated with the administration of large households, such as Anne Hutchinson's in Alford, could be considerable. This was especially true in the event of the absence or death of their husbands, in which case women often assumed complete charge. Within the family, mothers consistently had a large and often equal part in arranging the marriages of their children, a role of importance in the shaping of family fortunes and influence as well as in providing for the happiness of children. Thus, in practice, there were frequent exceptions to a theory and a legal structure that nonetheless remained firmly in place and, if challenged, usually prevailed.

For seventeenth-century Puritan women from New England, the realities of life were even further removed from the confines of traditional patriarchy. Both their religious tradition and the responsibilities they assumed as participants in the founding of a frontier society meant that their sense of self and the attitudes of others toward them were multifaceted.

In sixteenth- and seventeenth-century England, two developments brought about a perceptible change in attitude about the personhood of women. The first was the stress by Reformation theologians on the doctrine of the priesthood of all believers. By affirming the validity and crucial importance of each individual's own direct access to the channels of grace, this new emphasis had both a personal and a social impact. Every woman could treasure within herself, and be regarded by others as having, a unique relationship to God.

In addition, Puritan marriage doctrine further affirmed the personhood of women by subtly altering the relationship of the sexes. Roman Catholic marriage doctrine and the position of the Church of England, which in this respect was derived from it, held that the marriage union was one ordained by God for the primary purpose of procreation, as in Gen. 1:28: "Be fruitful and multiply." A secondary purpose for both was the companionship of husband and wife, the "mutual society" of husband and wife of the Book of Common Prayer and the corresponding Catholic doctrine of "fides."[63] Puritan marriage doctrine, on the other hand, was rooted in Genesis 2:18, a different text that pointed to a different primary purpose for marriage: "Then the Lord God said, 'It is not good that man should be alone, I will make him a helper for his partner.'" The first purpose of marriage thus became for the Puritans not procreation but companionship, and procreation became secondary.[64] The rite that united the partners became a covenant, no longer a sacrament as it was for the Roman church. Within the covenant, the emphasis on the mutuality of the bond of love that united the two partners enhanced the integrity of both. It was a covenant entered into by two consenting adults who promised each other and God always to love one another. To break the covenant was to deny one's commitment to God. To love and respect one another was to do God's will. "They stretched their souls . . . to love in the spirit of godliness," says one study of Puritan marriage, and "suffused marital relations afresh with religious emotion."[65] The commitment to love that was part of the marriage covenant did not require romantic attachment (although married love often became romantic if parents had arranged a marriage wisely). It was rather a deep good will springing from God's love that was required. A contemporary tract entitled *The Well Ordered Family* put it this way:

> *Husbands and wives [are] to have and manifest very great affection, love and kindness to one another. They should (out of con-*

science to God) study and strive to render each others life easy,
quiet and comfortable; to please, gratify and oblige one another,
as far as lawfully they can. [66]

Within such a bond, the performance of the many duties belonging to
marriage ideally became agreeable and easy.

Married life was a disciplined one with clear obligations for both
partners. The primary obligation of sexual union was one to be imbued
with both tenderness and pleasure. Sexual passion was affirmed as part
of God's almighty plan, and like the rest of his creation, it was good,
as long as it never became so consuming as to eclipse its Creator.
Thomas Shepard experienced in his marriage a passion that made him
uneasy. When Margaret Shepard bore his eldest son, she was in labor
for four days, and he agonized over her pain and danger: "The Lord did
teach me much by it and I had need of it, it for I began to grow secretly
proud and full of sensuality delighting my soul in my dear wife more
than in my God whom I had promised better unto" (57).

The promise of both partners to live together in peace and fidelity
was an equally important part of the covenant, and it shaped the well-
defined marital division of labor, which was rooted in a long English
tradition. The husband, as the ultimate authority, was to provide for
the family and supervise the religious education and discipline of the
household. Although the wife was to obey her husband and accept his
direction in all things, she was also given important direct authority
beneath him enabling her to work with him for the good of the family.
She was to nurture children and take responsibility for their earliest
training and education. As we have seen, she also managed the household herself or directed others (children, apprentices, and servants) at
the tasks of baking, sewing, weaving, churning, scrubbing, and all the
rest. She was called upon to emulate and was frequently eulogized as
showing forth the qualities of the "virtuous woman" of Proverbs
31:10–31, who not only served her husband and children with industry and joy, but who was also "a woman who fears the Lord."[67]

Sometimes, as a recent study suggests, this very selflessness of
women proved to be a source of indirect authority beyond the direct
authority that they exercised over children and household. In a soci-

ety that had made female submissiveness and generosity of spirit an article of faith, the more a woman excelled in her role as helpmeet,
mother, and manager, the more she was likely to be admired and
listened to. Both Anne Hutchinson and Anne Bradstreet grounded
their authority and found their appeal in part through their articulated stances as "virtuous" women. Anne Hutchinson's detractors, of
course, held that she had far overstepped the bounds of her assigned
role, but her supporters praised her for her selflessness in family and
community as much as for her spiritual power. Bradstreet consistently
celebrated the joy and the comfort that she found through mingling
her role as adoring and generous wife and mother with a similarly generous submission to God.[68]

Beyond the mitigating effect that Reformation theology and Puritan marriage doctrine had on the inferior position of seventeenth-
century English and New English women, the physical realities of life
in New England provided an even more positive environment. It was
not a situation that persisted when the society had become more settled; but in the earliest years, a number of circumstances contributed
to the welfare of New England women.

Demography was in their favor. There were simply fewer women
than men, a situation that gave them a kind of bargaining power. For
example, parents could be more selective in the choice of a husband
who would be truly suited to their daughter and provide well for her.
The need during the earliest New England years for the family to be a
self-sufficient economic unit, producing all that it needed, meant that
the role of women in the home was of crucial importance and, therefore, probably more highly valued. The legal position of New England
women improved too, partly because of the unsystematic application
of English law in a new situation. Some protection of women's property, for example, began to appear in the guise of prenuptial agree-
ments giving them some control over their dowries, although no law
established such a right. And New England women were healthier
than their English sisters. The standard of living was higher in the Bay
Colony, and, as English visitors noted, both men and women ate more
and lived longer.

A final circumstance that greatly improved the quality of life for

New England women was the moral tone of the society. The atmosphere was perhaps oppressive, but it did increase the security of women. Enormous social, legal, and ecclesiastical pressure kept marriages stable. For a time, at least, there was virtually no double standard of behavior for men and women since adultery was as serious a crime for a man as for a woman. And in the first few decades, there was no prostitution in Massachusetts.

The role of women in the churches of New England was made up of a patchwork of these complex and at times conflicting social and religious forces. Paralleling their lack of participation in the affairs of society, there is no surviving evidence of any regular participation by women in the governance of the churches.[69] There is, indeed, no mention of women in congregational church documents from the treatises of Robert Browne (the earliest English promulgator of congregational principles) to the Cambridge Platform of Church Discipline of 1648, because their invisibility in the structures of power was a given of their society. The Cambridge Platform speaks of "ordinary church power" (as opposed to the extraordinary power of apostles, prophets, and evangelists) as belonging "unto the brotherhood."[70] To have included the sisterhood in church governance would have been to go against nearly universal social attitudes, habits, and convictions. Reinforcing accepted practice and giving it an additional religious aura was the biblical injunction from 1 Timothy 2:11–12: "Let a woman learn in silence with full submissiveness. I permit no woman to teach or to have authority over a man; she is to keep silent."

The nominal exception to the lack of assigned church roles for women was the position of "widow" derived from a literal reading of 1 Timothy 5:9–10. The designation appears in English congregational writings and in the Cambridge Platform, where provision is made for the appointment of "ancient widows (where they may be had) to minister in the church, in giving attendance to the sick, and to give succor unto them."[71] The position never materialized in any significant form in New England, partly because the specifications listed in the biblical passage narrowed the field of possible candidates almost to extinction. To qualify, a woman must be over sixty, have been married only once, have raised a family, and "have diligently followed every good work."

To be denied participation in the governance of a congregational church as these women were would seem today to be a severe disability. Participation is, after all, the essence of congregationalism. It is what strengthens and builds up the body of Christ. The company of men who came to Massachusetts Bay deemed it a high privilege to gather churches; to elect and ordain pastors, elders, and deacons; to receive new members; to discipline old members; and to contribute to the maintenance of the church. One must wonder how women felt about being excluded from all of this. They were, of course children of their time, and accordingly many of them may have believed that they were indeed incapable of such responsibility.

In contrast, the spiritual life of New England churches offered women a level of participation previously unknown to them in their English church experience. The revival atmosphere of the first years in New England and the heightened spiritual awareness it engendered greatly attracted women. The call to open oneself to the Spirit and to search for an encounter with God provided an immediate sense of personal worth and, for some, an accompanying desire for personal witness. This incipient enthusiasm was intensified by the surge of radical spirituality associated with the Antinomian Controversy.

John Winthrop noted the way in which the antinomians "commonly labored to work first upon women, being (as they conceived) the weaker to resist; the more flexible, tender, and ready to yield; and if once they could wind [entice] in them, as by an Eve, to catch their husbands also."[72] And Thomas Shepard accused Hutchinson herself, in her church trial, of being one who was "likely with her fluent tongue and forwardness in expressions to seduce and draw away many, especially simple women."[73] Present-day scholars concur in finding in radical Puritanism a special attraction for women as well as a vehicle for their creativity. It was, at least in part, a "women's movement."[74]

Those early years provided opportunities for women, too, since the church community allowed a certain amount of informality and flexibility, opening up avenues for self-expression and leadership that demanded no formal education and that were, therefore, accessible to all. Meetings such as Anne Hutchinson's were possible in those days. The opportunity for public self-expression in the church for men and women alike was, of course, both limited and short-lived, virtually ending in the Bay Colony with the suppression of the Hutchinsonians. The spirituality that gave birth to it, however, continued to be an important part of the ethos of all New England churches and found its chief expression in the public declaration of faith required of each prospective member.

Although there were a few women (and a few men) who felt too shy to speak in public and were allowed to make their confessions privately to the minister, most joined with the congregation in telling their stories of the Spirit. They very likely found it an experience that knit them to the fellowship more closely, "for the increase of their love to those that join them," as Shepard had said.[75] The experience may also have increased the self-confidence of many women, since it was an act into which each woman entered, not as a dependent, as she almost always was otherwise, but as a unique child of God. As a child of God, she knew that she was valued and held in respect by all of the other members of the body of Christ.

THE PASTOR

Thomas Shepard's *Autobiography, Journal,* and most of his sermons provide abundant evidence of unquestioning participation in the attitudes and practices of his time with regard to the position of women. However, the *Autobiography* and *Journal* also reveal a man who, although molded by his society and his education, was perhaps unusually sensitive to the spirituality and personhood of women, at least with regard to the two women who as wives shared his adult life and about whom he wrote.[76]

Shepard nowhere addresses the issue of the nature and role of women (or of men) directly because, like his contemporaries, he believed that God had given these roles as part of the natural order and that they were, therefore, not in the least controversial or a subject for more than passing notice. His attitudes can be found, however, in parenthetical remarks, analogies, and illustrations throughout his theological writings. In an essay on "The Church Membership of Children," Shepard speaks of the accepted role of women in church polity as in practice somewhat analogous to the situation of children as members. He asserts that a child can be a church member and still be excluded from the Lord's Supper, because, as in the case of women,

> *there is a plain difference between member and member (though professing believers) in point of privilege, though they lie under no sin; for a man may speak and prophesy in the church, not women. A company of men may make a church, and so receive in and cast out of the church, but not women, though professing saints.* [77]

In this passage Shepard is speaking of congregational polity rather than the nature of women; elsewhere he links the two. In a reference to the "working of miracles" and the "preaching of sermons," he adds parenthetically, "which women are not regularly capable of."[78]

When we turn to Shepard's commitment to Puritan marriage doctrine as expressed in his sermons, women, despite their limited role, begin to appear as persons. In a series of sermons preached in Cambridge soon after his arrival there, Shepard compares the love of Jesus for each person to the love of husband for wife. The passage begins with a call to be open to Christ's perfect love. As the qualities of that love are described, an analogy with the less perfect love of a man for a woman unfolds:

> *Consider it is nothing else but love the Lord looks for. . . . Love looks for nothing else but love . . . he desires only love, only thy heart. . . . Consider what he will do for thee, how he will love thee, if thou wilt thus love him. . . .*
>
> *He will enrich thee. As it is with man and wife, all that he has is hers. . . .*

*He will dwell with thee as a man must dwell with his wife.
. . . If he does depart he will not be long, but return again. . . .*

*He will rejoice in thee and over thee . . . as a bridegroom does
over the bride. . . .*

*He will exceedingly comfort thee; and look as it is with tender
husbands, then they comfort most when most sorrows be-
tide. . . .*

*No sin shall part thee and him. . . . If a husband marries a
woman only for so long as she is in health, then when sickness
comes he may depart; but e contra . . . nothing but adultery can
part. . . . for nothing breaks till [the] covenant is broken. . . .*

*Death cannot [part thee and him]. It must part man and wife,
though loved never so dearly before.*[79]

Here is the commitment to a shared life, to fidelity, companionship,
forgiveness, tenderness, and rejoicing in one another.

In his second wife, Joanna Hooker, Shepard found, and to some extent created, the ideal Puritan wife. The eldest daughter of Thomas
Hooker, she had undoubtedly been raised to show forth the feminine
virtues of sacrifice, industry, and love. She had known Shepard all of
her life as her father's student, dear friend, and respected colleague. It
was natural, when Shepard became a widower, that her loving parents,
with her best interest at heart should have arranged a marriage to him.
Since she cannot have been more than sixteen years old when they
were married, in 1637, she was still part child when she traveled from
Hartford to Cambridge to begin married life.[80] Shepard's influence must,
therefore, have molded her further into the woman of grace and piety
that he remembered her to have been. After nine years of marriage, she
died in childbirth at the age of twenty-five. Shepard concluded his
Autobiography with an encomium expressive of what she had meant to
him, in words that echo the writer of Proverbs. Even if one allows for
the Puritan habit of eulogy, it is a moving testament of respect and tenderness from which at least the outlines of a credible person emerge:

She was a woman of incomparable meekness of spirit, toward myself especially, and very loving, of great prudence to take care for and order my family affairs, being neither too lavish nor sordid in anything so that I knew not what was under her hands. She had an excellency to reprove for sin and discerned the evils of men. She loved God's people dearly and [was] studious to profit by their fellowship, and therefore loved their company. She loved God's word exceedingly and hence was glad she could read my notes which she had to muse on every week. She had a spirit of prayer beyond ordinary of her time and experience. She was fit to die long before she did die. . . but her work not being done . . . she lived almost nine years with me and was the comfort of my life to me, and the last sacrament before her lying in seemed to be full of Christ and thereby fitted for heaven. She did oft say she should not outlive this child, and when her fever first began. . . she told me so, that we should love exceedingly together because we should not live long together. . . . The night before she died. . . she knew none else so as to speak to them, yet she knew Jesus Christ and could speak to him, and therefore . . . she broke out into a most heavenly, heartbreaking prayer after Christ, her dear redeemer, for the spirit of life, and so continued praying until the last hour of her death. (73)

As is evident here, although Joanna was meek and dutiful and practiced a piety guided by her husband, she also loved with spontaneity and was possessed of a faith that filled Shepard with awe.

Shepard's relationship to his first wife was quite different. As we have seen, he met and married Margaret Touteville while he served as chaplain to Sir Richard Darley of Buttercrambe in Yorkshire. Theirs was not an arranged marriage but a love match between adults. We have seen Shepard "delighting " his "soul in [his] dear wife more than in [his] God."[81] Margaret, too, was "incomparably loving" to him (55). Their relationship seems, in addition, to have been one of near equality in terms of emotional interaction and mutual respect. Shepard notes in the scattered but deeply felt references to Margaret in his

Autobiography not just her piety and devotion to him, but also what she thought and how she felt. The chaotic, hunted life that they were launched upon made her in one instance "full of fears," but she was also a woman of spirit and independent mind who shared Shepard's commitment to Puritan values. This made her a steadying companion for Thomas during the dark and lonely months in Northumberland. "God comforted us" there, he remembered later, "in our solitary and yet married condition" (56). Margaret participated in making the crucial decisions that determined their joint future. Soon after they were married, they decided to leave Yorkshire—partly because of the changed political climate but also because "she was unwilling to stay at Buttercrambe," perhaps wanting independence from the Darley household (55). Later, when they struggled with the decision to emigrate to New England, she was eager to go and, says Shepard, "put me on to it" (58). Still later, after the death of one infant and the birth of another, after fleeing and hiding and near shipwreck, when they finally arrived safely in New England, her commitment to the Puritan vision was still shining. She rejoiced, Shepard remembered, that he was now delivered "from the hand of my enemies and among God's people, and also the child under God's precious ordinances" (66). She died four months later after a long illness, but not before joining in the rite that was for her the fulfillment of the hope that had sustained them through such suffering. On the day that the church in Cambridge was gathered Shepard and some other new members came to her sick chamber to receive her into fellowship with them. Shepard described the moment: "For the Lord hereby filled her heart with such unspeakable joy and assurance of God's love, that she said to us she had now enough; and we were afraid her feeble body, would at that time have fallen under the weight of her joy."[82]

THE CONFESSIONS

In turning from Shepard's expressed attitudes about women to their own voices as recorded by him one enters a complex and difficult genre. It is important, first of all, to note that the confessions are his records and, therefore, his interpretation of what was said.[83] Judging from their abbreviated and often fragmentary character, they were probably either recorded in the meetinghouse at the moment of confession or, in the case of some that appear to have been copied, incorporated into the notebook later from original notes. Shepard's intent seems to have been to preserve for church records lively evidence of the "visible faith" of his flock.[84] The influence of his own personality is, therefore, probably minimal in the words he preserved. Another and more formidable difficulty is the nature of the two manuscripts that resulted from the haste of transcription. Scattered through as they are with incomplete sentences, abbreviations, irregular punctuation, frequent changes of person and of tense, they are difficult to read and even more difficult to interpret. Nonetheless, if we approach them with care and imagination, it is possible to hear at least snatches of these voices from the past.

In most respects the narratives of men and women appear to have been delivered and recorded in a similar fashion. Two differences in the text are probably due more to the social situation of women than to any intent of Shepard's. The women's confessions are, in general, shorter than the men's—a fact probably attributable to their timidity in the unfamiliar and highly ambiguous situation in which they found themselves as believers ordinarily asked to "keep silent" in church meetings but on this one, significant occasion, urged to public confession. There is, in addition, a difference in their designation as speakers that clearly indicates their subordinate social status. Men are designated by full names or by title such as "Goodman Fessington" or "Mr. Dunster." Women, except in the case of two out of thirty-one confessions, are identified by their relationship to a male family member or to an employer, as in "Goodwife Willows," "Eliz[abeth] Dunster, Sister to Brother Dunster," "John Sill His Wife," or "Brother Jackson's Maid." In this Shepard was, of course, adhering to customary usage. He seems generally to have treated the women penitents in his flock with the same courtesy and seriousness as the men. His respect for their individual integrity as believers appears especially in the fact that husbands and wives did not necessarily join the church on the same occasion, indicating that women as well as men were encouraged to make their confessions when ready and moved by the Spirit to do so. Brother Crackbone's wife, for example, did not join the church until four years after her husband, Gilbert; Jane Holmes became a member about two years before her husband, Robert. Thomas Bridge apparently never joined the church at all, although his wife, Dorcas, made her confession and was accepted in 1648.[85]

Although the spirituality of men and women differed in some respects, which will be considered below, their most basic values as expressed in these confessions were held in common. Later in the century, there are signs of the emergence of a peculiarly female piety, recently identified by scholars as one that tended to set women apart and surround them with an aura of purity, fragility, and special closeness to God.[86] There are some indications of the seeds of such a development in these testaments, but it had not yet taken shape among the first generation of colonial women. "In a very real sense," writes one scholar, "there is no such thing as *female* piety in early New England . . . the same Christ-like bearing was required of both male and female."[87]

Most of the women in the narratives Shepard recorded came to New England with their husbands, although some came as young people with their parents or as servants, and a few more as widows with children. Whatever their situation, it is evident from their confessions that they came for the same reasons as the men: to participate in God's true and pure church, to help to create a Zion in the wilderness, and to enhance their own spiritual welfare and that of their children by their commitment to the Puritan vision. A majority of both sexes found, in addition, that the experience of emigration and resettling was a trauma that, at least initially, shook their faith.

Also similar throughout the collection are the underlying theological and psychological assumptions that structure the confessions and form much of their content. Each one is fashioned, at least to some degree, after the traditional *ordo salutis,* which had been absorbed from earliest childhood and greatly reinforced by the preaching and counseling of Thomas Hooker and Thomas Shepard. A few, especially those of the better-educated penitents, such as Nathaniel Eaton,

Henry Dunster, William Andrews, and Daniel Gookin, recount conversions detailing the classical steps of conviction, humiliation, and faith. Most, including all of the women, tell stories less theologically articulate; but all, as we have seen above, describe the struggle to attain the humiliation that Shepard preached so insistently as the necessary prelude to the advent of faith.

Finally, common to all of these confessions is the vital and pervasive evidence all through them of an intense and personal acquaintance with the Bible, which for all Protestant English people was the predominant literary as well as spiritual influence in their lives. The language in which the narratives of both men and women are expressed is saturated with the phrases and metaphors of the Bible. Not only were its phrases familiar from reading and rereading and from listening to sermons, but the Bible actually became for them a vehicle of the Spirit through the Word that it contained. To read the Bible, for these believers, was to be in contact with the Spirit (and nearly all first-generation Puritans were able to read if not to write).[88] They used the illumination of the Spirit as it came to them through prayerful reading, both as a metaphor through which they could interpret and find spiritual significance in the events of daily life and as an essential guide in negotiating the path toward grace. When Brother Crackbone's wife saw her house burn, for example, she transformed the experience into a metaphor for her own spirit: "And seeing house burned down . . . and as my spirit was fiery so to burn all I had, and hence prayed Lord would send fire of word, baptize me with fire [Matt. 3:11; Luke 3:16]. And since then Lord hath set my heart at liberty" (140).[89]

In their selection of biblical texts for inspiration and spiritual guidance through their difficult pilgrimage, most of these confessors chose a variety of texts without regard to gender. There are some, however, who chose passages that related rather explicitly to themselves as women or men, passages that were not chosen by the other sex. Only Nathaniel Eaton and William Ames, for example, fearfully identified their spiritual plight with the rejection of Esau in Genesis 27:1–41 (55, 211). Only Francis Moore feared that his repentance might be ineffectual like "the repentance of Cain and Judas" as described in Genesis 4:13–14 and Matthew 27:3–5 (36). Among the women, Mary Angier sought for hope in the story of the healing of "the woman with the bloody issue," recounted in Mark 5:25–34, Luke 8:43–48, and Matthew 9:20–22; and Jane Holmes alone in the confessions found encouragement in the "tokens" pledged by Judah to Tamar in Gen. 38:18–26 (67, 80).[90] In their choice of these gender-specific texts, both men and women entered even more deeply into a personal identification with the events and scenes of the Bible.

Beyond the clear patterns of similarity that run through the confessions of the men and women in Shepard's collection, there is a dimension in which both individuality and male and female variations emerge, despite the fact that the act of confession was not intended to be either creative or self-revelatory. It was a ritual act undertaken in a prescribed manner, the purpose of which was to show forth the reality of divine action upon an individual human soul as the necessary prelude to acceptance into the church of visible saints.[91] However, the act of confession is inevitably both personal and creative to some degree. Even when approached in the most formulaic manner, the selection of the fragments of one's past and their reconstruction into a coherent whole is a creative, even a "fictional" process.[92] If then, that creative act is understood to have been undertaken with great emotion and intensity of purpose because of its crucial importance to the present and future of the confessor, we can suspect that it may prove to be self-revelatory as well. It is not surprising, therefore, that in addition to conformity to the accepted order of salvation, the confessions of women also express the central paradox of their position in the church. They accepted a passive and obedient role at the same time that they asserted their spiritual equality before God by publicly telling their own stories of spiritual striving.

For these women, as for all people of faith, the most basic circumstances of their lives shaped their spirituality. Central to their experience from childhood to the grave was the reality of dependence upon men and, at least for some of them, a sense of inferiority that went with it. In many of their narratives, there is evidence of an implicit recognition and acceptance of physical, social, and emotional dependence.

At the time of their confessions, twenty-five of the thirty-one women were either married or widows.[93] Of these twenty-five, fourteen were married in England and eleven after arriving in New England. In the former group, there are indications of dependence not present in the confessions of the women who were married in New England. Simply by the frequent naming of fathers and especially husbands, they suggest dependence. Some references to husbands are unobtrusive parts of a narrative of spiritual events, such as the passing mention of marriage: "and so being married" or "God changed her estate." Others are clear statements about the authority of husbands, especially with regard to emigration to New England. "And so my husband's heart was inclined to come to New England," says Martha Collins, as an explanation for their departure. "Then I secretly desired it," she goes on, "but yet opposite I was to it by looking upon my miseries here" (131). Mary Angier Sparrowhawk, "when her husband was resolved to come...came to the ship thinking to get good," that is, spiritual good in a new life (66). Martha Collins was more ambivalent about the decision to emigrate, but both followed their husbands obediently. Four women in this group are exceptions to the pattern and do not mention their husbands: Mrs. Greene, Isabell Jackson, Joanna Sill, and Jane Stevenson. Mrs. Greene's confession is a fragment that was broken off apparently because of her timidity, and Shepard says, "testimonies [supporting evidence from the congregation] carried it" (118). Joanna Sill may have been an independent person from the beginning. She certainly became so, remaining a widow until her death more than twenty years after the death of her husband, managing the family estate, and receiving a land grant that enlarged it. Although Jane Stevenson arrived from England with her husband and one child, she lived most of her married life in Cambridge, where she bore seven more children. The numbers in this sample are too small to warrant any conclusion, but it is tempting to speculate that for the ten women who were married in New England, none of whom mentions her husband, as well as for Joanna Sill and Jane Stevenson, the demands and the opportunities of the wilderness experience gave them a new self-confidence and independence of spirit.

In contrast to the women, only five of twenty men who were married at the time of confession mention wives even in passing. Of those five, only William Manning refers to his wife in connection with the decision to emigrate: "my wife and I hearing some certainty of things here, I desired to come hither" (97). Although these numbers are again too small to draw any firm conclusion from them, it is interesting to note that the five men who refer to their wives were also married in England. Possibly the trauma of separation from families, of the frightening journey at sea, and of settling into an unfamiliar and harsh new life bound husbands and wives with special closeness.

Among the women who had been married in England, husbands also played a prominent part in their approach to God and in shaping the quality of their spirituality, as opposed to the complete absence in the male narratives of wives as having had any clear bearing on their religious consciousness. These women were sensitive to and influenced by the spiritual attitudes of their husbands. Some even looked to them for spiritual counsel. Martha Collins, for example, was led by a loving husband to the beginnings of a conversion experience: "by my husband's speaking I saw my original corruption and miserable condition and so had a hungering after means [of grace] which were most searching." A little later when her doubts remained, she refused to find comfort in his encouragement because she "thought it was his affection to me" (131). Mary Gookin, when her "heart was troubled, . . . thought [she] would speak to [her] husband" in her search for spiritual comfort.[94] Ann Errington and Jane Palfrey, on the other hand, seem almost painfully fearful of the judgment of their husbands. Errington was so lacking in self-confidence and cared so much what her husband thought of her spiritual condition that she confessed when self-confrontation was most painful, "I durst not tell my husband fearing he would loath me if he knew me" (185). And when Jane Palfrey Willows found herself "rebellious" and "discontented," she told the Cambridge congregation that she considered what a "woeful frame [of mind] I had distrusting in God's providence and so was in a confusion in my spirit and could not speak to my husband. So I went sadly loathing myself" (151).[95]

In the case of Goodwife Champney, spiritual and marital discontent are mingled. She seems to have secretly blamed her husband for her disappointment with New England. Having emigrated nourishing the hope that there she "should be drawn [to God]," she found instead that "when I was brought hither I was in some sadness and would not speak and hence [I was] in straits and discontent with my married condition" (191).

The close relationship between marital and spiritual emotion expressed in all of these narratives is one aspect of a more general characteristic discernible in the faith of many mid-seventeenth-century women. As some recent scholars have pointed out, their spirituality often reveals a blending of faith and sexuality. That is, their relationship to God resembles and, at times, in their language is nearly indistinguishable from their relationships to the men in their lives.[96] In addition, the virtues that they are urged to show forth as Christians are also the virtues of a good seventeenth-century wife: gentleness, wholehearted obedience, generous love, willing service, and the capacity to lose one's self in another and thereby find fulfillment. "Traditional female values," as one scholar has observed, were thus transformed into "spiritual strengths."[97]

In these Cambridge confessions, the tendency to blend faith with sexuality appears first of all in the occasional intertwining of spiritual and marital metaphors. When, after the death of her husband, Mistress Smith's "heart was sinking," she turned to God in language that expressed her rather specific longing: "the Lord helped me, Thy maker is thy husband [Isa. 54:5], and though hid. And the Lord made me set a higher price upon him than a husband."[98] Brother Jackson's Maid was even more concrete in her imagery as she was drawn toward faith believing that "Christ would be better than earthly husband. No fear there of widowhood" (120).

The quality of the humiliation that many women of different ages and marital status experienced, before receiving grace and the response of faith that followed it, reflect a similar mingling of faith and sexuality. As we have seen above, Shepard preached a radical humility that called for complete abandonment of self to God's will, even to damnation.[99] This kind of humility seems to have come more easily to women than to men. Joanna Sill "found it hard if the Lord should damn her and never show mercy yet to be content" but did find herself able to "let Him do what He would" (52). Mary Angier Sparrowhawk also came to feel that she could "let Him do what He will" (68). And Jane Holmes struggled in "seeking the Lord, to submit in anything to His will that if never show mercy yet I might submit and not blaspheme" (80). Having been taught the she must "lie under Lord if He would show mercy," Barbary Cutter knew also that she must in the absence of mercy, accept that God would "do what He would" (92).[100]

There are many examples among the male narratives of similar attitudes and metaphorical language. However, with the clear exception of Daniel Gookin, who speaks of a Lord who "made me contented to lie down at God's feet to be disposed of as God would," and perhaps of Jonathan Mitchel who mentions hearing "directions how to... come to him and let him do with thee what he will," the men do not seem to have experienced the radical degree of humiliation described by some of the women.[101] Interesting among the male narratives, however, are two descriptions of a turbulent despair in the face of their failure to find humiliation that have no female parallels. William Andrews "had oft temptation to kill myself hence durst not carry a knife about me nor go near water" (112). And Mr. Haynes feared lest he "lay violent hands on myself" (168). But these are examples of struggle, not of humiliation.

For many women, the response of faith that followed humiliation blended willing submission into the peace that followed conversion. Jane Palfrey was made by God's word "to lie down. And [I] entrusted the Lord to keep down my spirit and... I was made willing" (152). Mary Angier Sparrowhawk felt closer to God than Jane Palfrey Willows and less in awe in her submission. "I saw I had nothing [to gain] by quarreling but by being contented and that [I] was the clay and Lord [my] potter." "[I] saw such a suitableness between Christ and me," she said near the end of her confession (68–69). Elizabeth Cutter who was "encouraged to seek the Lord and to be content with His condemning will to lie at Lord's feet," eventually did find that she "desired Lord to teach me and desired to submit" (146). After she "came over seas" Elizabeth Dunster felt "assured I was where God would have me, and so I submitted."[102]

With regard to submission, there is a quite persistent difference of emphasis between the male and female narratives. Although there are many men who, like Francis Moore, speak of being "truly humbled," the word "submit" does not appear in any form in any male narrative in these collections (36). The difference in emphasis suggests at the very least that women found it easier than men to respond to the call that went out to both of them to become brides of Christ, with the kind of surrender that that involved. Certainly there is no man who responded with the alacrity of Brother Jackson's Maid who "took Christ . . . upon His own terms" when, as we have seen, she realized that "Christ would be better than earthly husband" (120). Nor is there a woman in this group who approached God with the challenge and self-confidence of John Stansby, who seized the biblical injunction and "went with boldness to the throne of grace" (87).

One final aspect of the spiritual narratives of these women is puzzling. Motherhood was as central to their lives and, therefore, one would presume, to their spirituality as was their position as wives. Students of Puritan female spirituality, beginning in the late seventeenth century with Cotton Mather and continuing into the present, have stressed the crucial importance of the childbirth experience and the extension of themselves in the careful nurture of children to the shaping of women as Christians. The pain and hazard of childbirth and the frequent experience of loss in the death of young children are said to have heightened the spiritual awareness of women and brought them closer to God. "They are in deaths so often," says Mather, "this prepares them to die, and this teaches them to live. . . . They are saved through childbearing; inasmuch as it singularly obliges them to continue in faith, charity and holiness, with sobriety."[103] Mather and others furnished examples from their pastorates of this awareness of women; the poet Anne Bradstreet wrote of it; Anne Hutchinson preached her message to women in childbirth.[104]

The evidence from many sources is abundant, but from this series of women's confessions it is meager. Among a minimum total of seventeen women with children, only four mention them at all. Of these four, all refer to the spiritual welfare of their children as a reason for emigration, as do the two men who mention their children. "Thinking that [my] children might get good it would be worth my journey," says Mary Angier (66). More fearfully and negatively, Ann Errington decided to come after "hearing children would curse parents for not getting them to means [of grace]" (185). Brother Crackbone's wife and Martha Collins alone speak more personally of turning to God as a response to the suffering or death of their children. When she saw, "afflictions on my child and took from me," Brother Crackbone's wife became "so troubled what [might become] of my children" and began to strive for faith more diligently and eventually to pray "to the Lord to make me fit for church fellowship and [the] Lord" (140). Martha Collins tells how when "one child was struck . . . I thought it was for my sin and so let the Lord do with me what He will" (131). These are moving testaments, but they are few. One wonders why. Did they feel constrained by public confession? Or was it, as one scholar has suggested, simply "the fact of America as a central, even obsessive concern of the imagination" that eliminated other metaphors and other personal preoccupations from the immediate concerns of both men and women?[105] Whatever the reason, at least in so far as their feelings were expressed in these confessions, the influence of husbands seems to have been more important than the experience of childbirth and loss in the conversion experience.

These are tentative voices that we have been listening to. They are whispers from the past, whose survival must be pondered and wondered at. They are, however, of real significance. Given the social and legal constraints that disabled seventeenth-century women, it is quite extraordinary that these New England women were encouraged to stand in a public forum and, on an apparently equal footing with men, recount an experience of grace that in all important respects was recognized as common to them both. It is a testament in part to the power of the Reformation emphasis on the biblical call to recognize each person as a unique child of God. It is also a testament to the power of the communal ideal of these early New Englanders. It was important to them that each member of the holy community—man or woman, servant or master—should contribute in his or her own way to the building up and sustaining of the body of Christ. Finally, the very existence of these women's confessions should make one alert to the extreme complexity of women's issues. It would be easy to assume in this instance that, because of the denial to women in the church of rights that we consider basic and because of their invisibility in most church records, they had virtually no role to play. The reality, however, is that their participation in such a significant part of the spiritual life of these churches was of great importance to their communities and to themselves.

The next three centuries would find women increasingly empowered by changes in the churches that had made that reality possible, changes in self-image and in communal attitude. An enhanced self-image was built, in particular, by the communal acceptance of their participation in the priesthood of all believers, which, as Williams has put it, "made women in at least the role of confessors, the spiritual equals of men."[106] It is not, however, an unambiguous story. Although the idea of spiritual equality appeared in radical Protestantism in the sixteenth century and was made more manifest in the seventeenth, three more centuries were to pass before the actual situation of women changed significantly. Churches have also contributed in important ways of their own to limiting the opportunities of women and to circumscribing their image.[107] They have tended to reinforce and often to sanctify the political and social constraints inhibiting the opportunities of women; and they have contributed to the isolation of women by insisting upon and idealizing their purity and essential passivity as wives and mothers. However, running through that checkered history is a continuum of respect for the personhood of women that is rooted in the gospel proclamation that "male and female" are "one in Christ Jesus" (Gal. 3:28) and that ultimately contributed to the sense of sisterhood and public self-confidence that have brought increasing freedom, equality, and self-realization in the nineteenth and twentieth centuries.

EPILOGUE

Thomas Hooker and Thomas Shepard died within two years of each other, Hooker in 1647 in Hartford and Shepard in 1649 in Cambridge. The passing of the founders was a pivotal event in the history of the church that had been gathered in Cambridge, marking and to some extent effecting a gradual departure from its original purity.

The church that Hooker and Shepard built with their parishioners had been fashioned out of their experience as Englishmen. In England they had been born, educated, and married. Hooker had raised five children there, and Shepard had left his firstborn son buried at Yarmouth. In England they had launched their ministries and put down deep roots among English people. But ultimately, they rebelled against their mother church and as a result were persecuted and rejected by the country that was their home. As part of a great migration, they came to New England bearing a glowing faith that had been forged in secret conventicles and fanned by persecution and that they, like most of their generation, believed to be the only perfect expression of God's will for humankind. This precious faith they brought to Cambridge, building a church that embodied and maintained its purity by including in its membership only those who had been touched by the Spirit. At mid-century, through their efforts, their church had become a stable and tightly knit body that still embodied that purity largely undiluted.

During the ministry of Jonathan Mitchel, who succeeded Shepard in 1650, the dilution began. Even in Shepard's time, the gradual increase of an alarming number of unconverted Christians had begun in the holy community. These unconverted souls were the children of first-generation members who had found themselves unable to testify to the experience of grace that was necessary for them to become full, communicant members. To make matters even worse, many of them had married and had children who could not be baptized, since baptism was a sacrament reserved for the children of church members only.

The Puritan clergy of the mid-seventeenth century attributed the falling-off of conversions to the selfishness and waywardness of a materialistic generation. Since then, scholars have suggested a variety of other possible explanations.[1] Perhaps most basic was a loosening of the church-centered bonds that had bound the first generation of settlers. As survivors of persecution and of a frightening sea voyage and as immigrants into a wilderness, they had had great need of one another. In the churches, the atmosphere of the first years had, therefore, been one of care and support as well as of strictness and purity. That atmosphere began to change as young people found new opportunities and began to free themselves from traditions that no longer seemed relevant and as they found themselves members of an increasingly thriving, secular society. The curtailment of the church members' role in the governance of the churches in the 1640s probably also played a part in lessening the involvement and commitment of their male parishioners. Perhaps most important of all was a paradox that lay at the heart of the self-image of first-generation Puritans. A rebellious, self-confident, courageous band, they praised each other for these qualities and taught their children to revere their character and their achievement. However, they made it a requirement of the wilderness Zion they had come to New England to build that its members should submit in obedience to the tenets of their theocratic ideal. These first-generation founders would not allow their children to be independent, passionate, and strong like themselves. At the same time, they blamed their children for their dependence and lack of commitment. Some of these young people yearned for a conversion experience but felt themselves unable to meet the standards of their parents. Others turned away to secular pursuits with less difficulty.

Toward the end of his ministry, Shepard had become concerned about the youth in his congregation. However, he asserted in a letter to an anxious friend shortly before his death that the baptized but unconverted children of church members should continue to be considered part of the church. After all, "the children of professing believers are in the same covenant God made with Abraham . . . for so the covenant runs, 'I will be thy God, and the God of thy seed.'" This means that there can be "no reason for any man to doubt of the salvation of his child if he dies, or that God will not do good to his child in time if he lives." A child can be cast out only if he "reject the gospel positively."[2] Shepard was extending a hand to the baptized but unconverted children of believers, but he failed to deal with the children of these children, who could not receive the seal of Abraham's covenant since their parents were unconverted. Thus began a long and increasing line of unbaptized and potentially disaffected Christians.

Jonathan Mitchel had fallen deeply under the influence of Shepard as a student at Harvard and sincerely wanted to emulate him. He was, nonetheless, a younger man with a different set of experiences, which made him more willing to recognize and adapt to the changes that were shaping his society. Although born in England, from his eleventh year he had been educated in New England, part of a new generation raised in firmly established churches that were feeling the pressures of an increasingly secular environment. By the end of the 1650s Mitchel had reluctantly but firmly committed himself to addressing the decline in church membership. Without discovering a way to keep these unconverted and unbaptized Christians "under those church-dispensations wherein grace is given, the church will die of a lingering, though not of a violent death," he feared. He urged his contemporaries to recognize what was happening:

> *The Lord hath not set up churches only that a few old Christians may keep one another warm while they live, and then carry away the church into the cold grave with them when they die; no, but that they might, with all the care, and with all the obligation, and advantages to that care that may be, nurse up still successively another generation of subjects to Christ that may stand up to him from one generation to another.*[3]

A battle was joined between proponents and opponents of compromise. In Mitchel's camp was Richard Mather, the sole member of the
first generation who stood for change. Firm in their commitment to an
unrevised Cambridge Platform were John Davenport; Charles Chaun-
cey, the president of Harvard; and, at least for a time, Increase
Mather, Richard's own son. A synod was called by the General Court,
which, after much heated debate, in June of 1662 produced a document popularly and derisively known as the "Half-Way Covenant."
Two crucial doctrines emerged in the compromise. Upholding the position of the founders was the affirmation that adult, unconverted
children of members, although they continue to be "under the watch,
discipline and government" of their church, "are not to be considered
full members admitted to the Lord's Supper." Bowing to the necessity
of making the path to church fellowship, if not church membership itself, less narrow, was the fifth proposition:

> Children of church members in covenant, who were admitted in
> minority [i.e., baptized], understanding the doctrine of faith,
> and publicly professing their assent thereto; not scandalous in
> life, and solemnly owning the covenant before the church,
> wherein they give up themselves and their children to the Lord,
> and subject themselves to the government of Christ in the
> church, their children are to be baptized.[4]

Mitchel guided his church to the adoption of the new propositions
in the belief that the compromise did preserve the heart of the ideal of
purity by continuing to deny the Lord's Supper to all who could not
testify to an experience of grace. From the time of the Half-Way Covenant, there were two covenants at the Church of Christ in Cambridge: one for full members and another, the "Covenant in Order to
their Children's being Baptized." Through the ministry of Nathaniel
Appleton, in the early nineteenth century, members were admitted by
both covenants.[5]

The adoption of the Half-Way Covenant is a fitting event with
which to conclude the story of the early history of the church that was

gathered in the Spirit in Cambridge. It marked and legitimized the dilution of the purity that had been so central to the church, especially under Thomas Shepard. In so doing, it altered both the idea of covenant and the ideal of the gathered church itself.

For the first generation of members of the Church of Christ at Cambridge, the covenant had been entered into as a response to conversion. It was the human response to the divine gift of the covenant of grace. The Half-Way Covenant was instead a rational covenant of promised commitment "to walk with God according to the rules of his holy word."[6] There had thus come to be a clear distinction between an internal, gracious covenant and an external, rational promise that Shepard might even have called a covenant of works.

Similarly, the ideal of a gathered church had begun to change. The church, which had been gathered in the Spirit in such a concrete way as to contain only those "visible saints" who had experienced God's grace, began a gradual transformation. The ideal of purity itself came under scrutiny even as it ceased to be a reality. By the end of the seventeenth century, in the pastorate of William Brattle, the requirement of a public "relation" for prospective members was discontinued. In its place a private examination by the pastor and elders to determine sincerity of commitment and orthodoxy of doctrine was substituted.

Today, in Cambridge, both the First Church in Cambridge, Unitarian Universalist, and the First Church in Cambridge, Congregational, United Church of Christ, are very far removed from the original "virgin" church from which they are descended. However, they both have recently affirmed their roots in their common ancestor and have at the same time made explicit a contemporary focus. The First Church, Unitarian Universalist, has replaced its nineteenth-century covenant with a new one that is an adaptation of the 1985 denominational "Principles and Purposes." In addition to explicit commitments to "promote . . . justice, equity, and compassion in human relations" and in the "world community," the covenant contains a grateful recognition of the sources of the "religious pluralism" from which the present "living tradition" of the church has been drawn. Among these are "wisdom from the world's religions," "Jewish and Christian teachings," "the guidance of reason," and in a final affirmation, the tradition in Cambridge where "the faithful keeping of. . . many generations, have sought to create in this place a beloved community of memory and hope."[7] At the First Church, Congregational, the sense of being gathered in the Spirit has remained at the heart of the church community as a specifically Christian awareness, but with a wide inclusiveness unknown to its predecessor. The recent adoption by the congregation of a "Covenant Testimony" of dedication to the pursuit of social justice and to peace through nonviolence followed from, but did not replace, the seventeenth-century covenant so long in use there. The testimony bears witness to a spiritual vitality that continues to shape the community. It can be seen as the product of a persistent effort to ponder and make explicit in the present the meaning and promise of the earlier covenant to "bind ourselves to walk in all our ways according to the rule of the Gospel."[8]

APPENDIX

Family Statistics for Women and Men Confessors in Shepard's Notebooks of Conversion Narratives

My statistics begin in every case with the information collected and sifted by Selement and Woolley in their Shepard's "Confessions" (see chapter 4, n. 8) and by McCarl in her "Shepard's Record of Relations" (see chapter 4, n. 19). Their information has been supplemented by reference to the following sources:

Banks, Charles Edward. *The Planters of the Commonwealth. . . 1620–1640*. Boston: Riverside Press, 1930.

———. *Topographical Dictionary of 2885 English Emigrants to New England, 1620–1650*, 3d ed. Baltimore: Genealogical Publishing Company, 1963.

Bridge, William F. *An Account of the Descendants of John Bridge, Cambridge, 1632*. Boston: J. S. Cushing and Co., 1884.

Farmer, John. *A Genealogical Register of the First Settlers of New England*. Lancaster, Mass.: Carter, Andrews and Co., 1829.

Gozzaldi, Mary Isabella. *Supplement and Index to Paige's History of Cambridge, Massachusetts*. Cambridge: Cambridge Historical Society, 1930.

Hotten, John Camden. *Original Lists of Persons of Quality, 1600–1700*. London: Chatt and Windus, 1874.

Paige, Lucius R. *History of Cambridge, Massachusetts, 1630–1877*. Boston: H. O. Houghton and Co., 1877.

Pope, Charles Henry. *The Pioneers of Massachusetts: A Descriptive List*. Baltimore: Genealogical Publishing Co., 1965.

Roberts, Gary Boyd, ed. *English Origins of New England Families from the New England Historical and Genealogical Register*, 1st ser., 3 vols. Baltimore: Genealogical Publishing Co., 1984. (Cited hereafter as NEHGR.)

Savage, James A. *Genealogical Dictionary of the First Settlers of New England*, 4 vols. Boston: Little, Brown, 1860.

Sharples, Stephen Paschall, ed. *Records of the Church of Christ at Cambridge in New England, 1632–1830*. Boston: E. Putnam, 1906.

WOMEN

Hannah ——— Brewer (or Anne)

Probably wife of John Brewer. Married in New England. Two children born in Cambridge (Selement and Woolley, 141).

Dorcas Downey (Dowing) Bridge

Married to Thomas Bridge in New England. Her husband came to New England as a teenager by 1632 with his brother and widowed father, John. Their only child born 2/16/49, about the time of her confession (McCarl, 439, 461; Paige, 500; Bridge, 10).

Goodwife Champney

Almost certainly Jane ———, wife of Richard Champney. Married in England. Came to New England on ship *Defense* with Thomas Shepard. Seven more children born in Cambridge (Selement and Woolley, 190).

Martha ——— Collins

Married in England. Came to Cambridge with husband, Edward, and four children. Four more children born in Cambridge (Selement and Woolley, 81, 130).

Elizabeth ——— Cooke

Probably married in New England since she was not listed among the passengers who came to New England in the Shepard party on the *Defense*. Her husband, Joseph, and brother-in-law, George, were listed for disguise purposes as servants of Roger Harlakenden. Her absence in the list is significant since the names of other wives and children in the Shepard party do appear. Five children born in Cambridge (McCarl, 439; Banks, *Planters*, 168; Hotten, 100; Paige, 513–14.

Brother Crackbone's Wife

Married to Gilbert Crackbone in England. Came to Cambridge with one or two children. Probably one or two more children born in Cambridge (Selement and Woolley, 139; Paige, 518).

Barbary Cutter
Unmarried at time of confession (Selement and Woolley, 89).
Elizabeth ——— Cutter
Married to William Cutter in England who came to New England
with their three children. She followed shortly (Selement and Wool-
ley, 144).
Elizabeth Dunster
Unmarried at time of confession. Had recently arrived in New England
(McCarl, 440; NEHGR, vol. I, 9).
Ann Errington
Widow who brought children Abraham (see below) and Rebecca with
her to Cambridge. Did not remarry (Selement and Woolley, 184;
Paige, 540; Sharples, 17).
Mary Dolling Gookin
Married in England. Came to Cambridge with husband, Daniel, and
three children. One child born in Virginia, two in Boston, and eight
more in Cambridge (McCarl, 438–39; Paige, 561, 563; Pope, 193).
Brother Greene's Wife
Probably Jane Banbridge Greene, almost certainly married in New En-
gland. Seven children born in Cambridge beginning in 1640, about the
time of her confession (Selement and Woolley, 117; Paige, 567).
Mrs. Greene
Probably Ellen ———, wife of Percival. Married in England. Two chil-
dren born in Cambridge (Selement and Woolley, 117; Paige, 567).
Mary ——— Griswald
Married to Francis Griswald in Cambridge. Three children born in
Cambridge (Selement and Woolley, 187).
Jane ——— Holmes
Married to Robert Holmes in Cambridge. Nine children born in Cam-
bridge (Selement and Woolley, 76).
Brother Jackson's Maid
Probably a widow. Name unknown (Selement and Woolley, 119).
Goodwife Jackson
Probably Isabell ———, first wife of Richard Jackson. May have been
married in England, since Richard was fifty-four years old in 1636
when he first appears as selectman. No children (McCarl, 436; Paige,
592).

Elizabeth Olbon Luxford
> Just married or soon-to-be married at time of confession. Two children born in Cambridge (Selement and Woolley, 38–39; Paige, 600).

Brother Moore's Wife
> Probably Joan ———, widow of John Champney. Married to Champney in England or soon after arrival in New England. Three children by Champney, three by Moore (Selement and Woolley, 122, 133).

Elizabeth Oakes (probably Elizabeth Fanning or Fenn)
> Unmarried. Adopted by Oakes family (McCarl, 435–36).

Mary Danforth Parish
> Married to Thomas Parish in New England. Three children (Selement and Woolley, 136).

Joanna ——— Sill
> Married in England to John Sill. Two children born in England. Never remarried after death of husband. Widow for at least twenty years (Selement and Woolley, 44, 49).

Sarah Smith
> Widow of Samuel Smith of Salem/Wenham. Widow with children married to widower Smith. There were children from her first marriage, stepchildren from marriage to Smith, and two more children by Smith. First marriage probably in England (McCarl, 440, 464; Pope, 423).

Mary Angier Sparrowhawk
> Married to Nathaniel Sparrowhawk in England. Came to Cambridge with husband and one child. Five more children born in Cambridge (Selement and Woolley, 62, 65).

Alice ——— Stedman
> Married John Stedman in Cambridge. Three children (Selement and Woolley, 72, 102).

Jane ——— Stevenson
> Married Andrew Stevenson in England. Came to New England with husband and one child. Seven more children born in Cambridge (McCarl, 436).

Elizabeth Stone
> Unmarried at time of confession. Fourth child of Gregory Stone, born 3/6/29 (McCarl, 440; Gozzaldi, 710).

Frances ——— Usher
> Married to Hezakiah Usher. Reference to mother in confession suggests

marriage in New England. Two children born in Cambridge, two more in Boston (Selement and Woolley, 182–83).

Jane Wilkinson Winship
Wife of Edward Winship. Probably married in New England. Four children born in Cambridge (Selement and Woolley, 147; Paige, 691, 695).

Jane Palfrey Willows
Widow, arrived in Cambridge with two children. Married George Willows in Cambridge. Two more children (Selement and Woolley, 150).

Men

William Andrews
Married to Mary ———— in England. One child born in England. Mary died January, 1640. Remarried to Reanna James the following August. Confession made in same year (Selement and Woolley, 110; Paige, 480).

William Ames
Unmarried at time of confession (Selement and Woolley, 209–10).

Abraham Arrington (Errington)
At time of confession either unmarried or just married to Rebecca Cutler. Six or seven children (McCarl 436–37; Paige, 541; Gozzaldi 241; Pope, 158; Sharples, 21).

Robert Browne
Unmarried at time of confession. Made freeman 5/2/49, indicating that he was a church member by that date. Married Barbara Eden 5/8/49 (McCarl, 437; Pope, 74).

Christopher Cane
Unmarried or just married to Margery ———— at time of confession. First child born 3/27/40. Four more children (Selement and Woolley, 58; Paige, 506; Sharples, 20).

Edward Collins
See Martha Collins above.

Richard Cutter
Unmarried at time of confession (Selement and Woolley, 178).

Robert Daniel
Married to Elizabeth ———— in England or shortly after emigration. No children at time of confession (Selement and Woolley, 60; Pope, 130).

Henry Dunster
>About to be married to widow Elizabeth Glover at time of confession (Selement and Woolley, 155; Paige, 537).

Nathaniel Eaton
>Married in England. Came to Cambridge with wife and several children (Selement and Woolley, 53; Paige, 539).

Richard Eccles
>Probably not yet married to Mary ———— at time of confession before 5/18/42 when he was made freeman. First child born 3/15/45. Three more children (Selement and Woolley, 44; Paige, 540).

John Fessenden
>Married to Jane ———— in England. No children (Selement and Woolley, 175).

John Furnell (Fownell)
>Married to Mary ———— in England. At least one child born in Cambridge (Selement and Woolley, 203; Paige, 547).

Daniel Gookin
>See Mary Dolling Gookin above.

Edward Hall
>Married to Margaret ———— probably in England. No children (Selement and Woolley, 31; Paige, 570).

William Hamlet
>Probably unmarried at time of confession (Selement and Woolley, 125).

Roger Haynes
>Unmarried at time of confession (Selement and Woolley, 165).

Robert Holmes
>See Jane Holmes above.

Sr. Jones
>Probably John Jones, unmarried at time of confession (Selement and Woolley, 198).

William Manning
>Married in England. One child born in England (Selement and Woolley, 93).

Jonathan Mitchell (Mitchel)
>Unmarried at time of confession (McCarl, 439).

Francis Moore
>Married in England. Came to Cambridge with wife, Katherine ————,

and two children. Two more children born in Cambridge (Selement and Woolley, 35).

Golden Moore
Probably unmarried at time of confession (Selement and Woolley, 122; Paige, 611).

Mr. Sanders
Perhaps Robert Sanders or Daniel Saunders. No biographical information (Selement and Woolley, 70).

Edward Shepard
Married to Violet ———— in England. Emigrated with three children, a fourth born in Cambridge (Selement and Woolley, 172).

John Shepard
Unmarried at time of confession made between 5/10/48 and 9/11/48. Married Rebecca Greenhill 10/4/49. Eleven children (McCarl, 436, 443; Paige, 654).

John Sill
See Joanna Sill above.

Abram Smith (Abraham)
No available information on marriage or children (McCarl, 439) Pope places him on ship *Planter,* in 1635 with wife, Alice, and child (418), information I have not been able to substantiate in Banks, Savage, or Farmer.

Nathaniel Sparrowhawk
See Mary Angier Sparrowhawk above.

John Stansby
No available information on marriage or children. Correspondence at the time of emigration suggests that he was unmarried in 1636 (Selement and Woolley, 85).

Sir Starr
Probably Comfort Starr (son of Comfort Starr, surgeon). Unmarried at time of confession (McCarl, 440).

John Stedman
Married in England to Alice ————. Three children born in Cambridge (Selement and Woolley, 72–73).

John Trumbull
Unmarried or just married to Elizabeth ———— at time of confession (Selement and Woolley, 106; Paige, 672).

George Willows
    See Jane Palfrey Willows above.
Nicholas Wyeth
    Married in England. Emigrated with wife and two children. Third child
    born in Cambridge and died at time of confession (Selement and Wool-
    ley, 192, 195).
Anonymous
    No available information. Internal evidence about influence of parents
    suggests that confessor was a young man, unmarried (Selement and
    Woolley, 205–6).

NOTES

FOREWORD

1. Thomas Hooker, "Spiritual Munition: A Funeral Sermon, June 22, 1626," in George H. Williams, Norman Pettit, Winfried Herget, and Sargent Bush, Jr., *Thomas Hooker: Writings in England and Holland, 1626–1633* (Cambridge: Harvard University Press, 1975), 44.

CHAPTER 1

1. Albert Peel, ed., *The Second Parte of a Register* (Cambridge: Cambridge University Press, 1915), 1:86. Quoted in Edmund S. Morgan, *Visible Saints: the History of a Puritan Idea* (New York: New York University Press, 1963), 14.

2. Covenant of the First Church in Charlestown, Massachusetts, 1630, used in worship at the First Church in Cambridge, Congregational, UCC, since its adoption in the pastorate of Alexander McKenzie (1867–1912). In Alexander McKenzie, *Lectures on the History of the First Church in Cambridge* (Boston: Congregational Publishing Society, 1873), 269–70.

3. David D. Hall, *Worlds of Wonder, Days of Judgment: Popular Religious Belief in Early New England* (New York: Alfred A. Knopf, 1989), 94. My interpretation in this section is much indebted to Hall's analysis in chap. 2.

4. Stephen Foster, *The Long Argument: English Puritanism and the Shaping of New England Culture, 1570–1700* (Chapel Hill and London: University of North Carolina Press, 1991), 5. For a discussion of the Reformed consensus, see David D. Hall, "Understanding the Puritans," in Stanley N. Katz, ed., *Colonial America: Essays in Politics and Social Development* (Boston: Little, Brown and Co., 1971), 31–50; and Dewey D. Wallace, Jr., *Puritans and Predestination: Grace in English Protestant Theology, 1525–1695* (Chapel Hill: University of North Carolina Press, 1982), especially 3–55.

147

5. John Calvin, *Institutes of the Christian Religion*, trans. John Allen (Philadelphia: Presbyterian Board of Publication, 1841), 1:188.

6. See Michael McGiffert, "Grace and Works: The Rise and Division of Covenant Divinity in Elizabethan Puritanism," *Harvard Theological Review* 75 (1982), 463–502, for an analysis of the development of two covenants in Reformation theology.

7. Cotton Mather, *Magnalia Christi Americana or the Ecclesiastical History of New England* (Hartford: Silas Andrus and Son, 1820), 1:250.

8. "The Canons of 1604," quoted in Christopher Hill, *Society and Puritanism in Pre-Revolutionary England*, 2d ed. (New York: Schocken Books, 1967), 301–2.

9. W. H. Frere and C. E. Douglas, eds., "A Survey of the Booke of Common Prayer," *Puritan Manifestoes: A Study of the Origin of the Puritan Revolt* (New York: E. S. Gorham, 1907), 71. Quoted in Horton Davies, *The Worship of the English Puritans* (Westminster: Dacre Press, 1948), 62, 68.

10. John Whitgift, *Works* (Cambridge: Cambridge University Press, 1853), 3:32. Quoted in Irvonwy Morgan, *The Godly Preachers of the Elizabethan Church* (London: Epworth Press, 1965), 26. Cartwright's comment came in the course of a controversy with Whitgift.

11. "Edmond Grindal to Queen Elizabeth I" (Dec. 8, 1576), Letter XXXIX in William Nicholson, ed., *The Remains of Edmond Grindal, D.D.* (Cambridge: Cambridge University Press, 1843), 387. Quoted in Christopher Hill, *The Collected Essays of Christopher Hill* (Amherst: University of Massachusetts Press, 1986), 2:69.

12. Robert Browne, *A Treatise of Reformation without tarying for anie, and of the wickedness of those Preachers which will not reforme till the Magistrate command or compell them* (Middleburgh, 1582). Quoted in William Haller, *The Rise of Puritanism, or, the Way to the New Jerusalem as Set Forth in Pulpit and Press from Thomas Cartwright to John Liliburne and John Milton, 1570–1643* (New York: Columbia University Press, 1938), 182.

13. Perry Miller, *Orthodoxy in Massachusetts, 1630–1650* (Cambridge: Harvard University Press, 1933), chap. 4.

14. Michael McGiffert, ed., *God's Plot: Puritan Spirituality in Thomas Shepard's Cambridge*, revised and expanded edition (Amherst: University of Massachusetts Press, 1994), 51.

15. Peter Heylyn, *Cyprianus Anglicus* (London: A. Seile, 1668), 539.

16. McGiffert, ed., *God's Plot*, 51.

17. Heylyn, *Cyprianus Anglicus*, 542; Sir Edward Dering quoted from Heylyn, 56, in Haller, *Rise of Puritanism*, 228.

18. William Laud, "Speech to Parliament" (March 12, 1644), in *The Autobiography of Dr. William Laud* (Oxford: John Henry Parker, 1839), 342.

19. William Laud, *The History of the Troubles and Tryal of the Most Reverend Father in God, William Laud Archbishop of Canterbury* in *The Works of Archbishop Laud* (Oxford: John Henry Parker, 1853), 3:408, 421. [Italics mine.]

20. Nicholas Tyacke, *Anti-Calvinists: The Rise of English Arminianism, c. 1590–1640* (Oxford: Clarendon Press, 1987), 7.

21. Francis Cheynell, *The Rise, Growth, and Danger of Socinianism* (London: Samuel Gellibrand, 1643), 63. Quoted in David D. Hall, *The Faithful Shepherd: A History of the New England Ministry in the Seventeenth Century* (Chapel Hill: University of North Carolina Press, 1972), 74.

22. At the suggestion of Anne Ferry, I have avoided using the term "Anglican" for this period of English history. With Ferry, Nicholas Tyacke holds that for the sixteenth and seventeenth centuries: "'Anglican'... is anachronistic to the point of being positively misleading" (Tyacke, *Anti-Calvinists*, viii). For other comments on the use of the term, see Paul Christianson, "Reformers and the Church of England under Elizabeth I and the Early Stuarts," *Journal of Ecclesiastical History* 31, no. 4, 463–82; and Patrick Collinson, "A Comment: Concerning the Name of Puritan," *Journal of Ecclesiastical History* 31, no. 4, 483–88.

23. Edward Cardwell, ed., *Documentary Annals of the Reformed Church of England*, 2d ed. (Oxford: Oxford University Press, 1844), 2:202. Quoted in Foster, *Long Argument*, 128.

24. Francis Quarles, *Divine Fancies* (London: n.p., 1632), Book I, Poem 33. Quoted in Paul S. Seaver, *The Puritan Lectureships: The Politics of Religious Dissent* (Stanford: Stanford University Press, 1970), 240.

25. Thomas Fuller, *History of the Worthies of England* (1662), ed. John Freeman (London: Allen and Unwin, 1952), 249.

26. McGiffert, ed., *God's Plot*, 58.

27. Andrew Delbanco, *The Puritan Ordeal* (Cambridge: Harvard University Press, 1989), 84.

28. John Winthrop, "A Model of Christian Charity," in Perry Miller, ed., *The American Puritans, Their Prose and Poetry* (Garden City, N.Y.: Doubleday, 1956), 82–83. Hugh J. Dawson in his "John Winthrop's Rite of Passage: The Origins of the 'Christian Charitie' Discourse," *Early American*

Literature 26, no. 3 (1991), 219–27, shows that Winthrop's homily was delivered in England prior to departure, probably in port aboard the *Arbella*.

29. James Kendall Hosmer, ed., *John Winthrop's Journal, "The History of New England," 1630–1649*, 2 vols. (New York: Barnes and Noble, Inc., 1946), 1:112. Quoted in Charles E. Hambrick-Stowe, *The Practice of Piety: Puritan Devotional Disciplines in Seventeenth Century New England* (Chapel Hill: University of North Carolina Press, 1982), 142.

30. See page 10.

31. Nathaniel Morton, *New England's Memoriall* (Cambridge, Mass.: John Usher, 1669), 75–76. Quoted in Morgan, *Visible Saints*, 83–84.

32. Hosmer, ed., *Winthrop's Journal*, 1:173–74.

33. Ibid., 1:116.

34. John Cotton, "A Sermon Delivered at Salem, 1636," in Larzer Ziff, ed., *John Cotton on the Churches of New England* (Cambridge: The Belknap Press of Harvard University Press, 1968), 57.

35. Charles Lloyd Cohen, *God's Caress: The Psychology of Puritan Religious Experience* (Oxford: Oxford University Press, 1986), 208.

36. Thomas Shepard, *The Sound Believer. Or, a Treatise of Evangelicall Conversion* (1645), in *The Works of Thomas Shepard* (Boston: Doctrinal Tract and Book Society, 1853), 1:196.

37. See Michael McGiffert, "Thomas Shepard: The Practice of Piety," in McGiffert, ed., *God's Plot*, 24; and Morgan, *Visible Saints*, 70.

38. Thomas Shepard, *The Parable of the Ten Virgins opened and applied: Being the Substance of Divers Sermons on Matth. 25:1–13* (1660), in *Works*, 2:65.

39. Bernard Bailyn, *The New England Merchants in the Seventeenth Century* (Cambridge: Harvard University Press, 1955), 16–23, 29–40.

40. Alexander Young, comp., *Chronicles of the First Planters of the Colony of Massachusetts Bay from 1623–1636* (Boston: Charles C. Little and James Brown, 1846), 427. Quoted in Larzer Ziff, *The Career of John Cotton, Puritanism and the American Experience* (Princeton: Princeton University Press, 1962), 58–59.

41. David D. Hall, ed., *The Antinomian Controversy, 1636–1638, a Documentary History*, 2d ed. (Durham and London: Duke University Press, 1990), 337.

42. John Cotton, *A Treatise of Faith*, n.d., 35, 14. Quoted in Norman Pettit, *The Heart Prepared: Grace and Conversion in Puritan Spiritual Life*, 2d ed. (Middletown, Conn.: Wesleyan University Press, 1989), 139.

43. John Cotton, *The Way of Life* (London: L. Fawne and S. Gellibrand,

1641), 277. Quoted in Philip F. Gura, *A Glimpse of Sion's Glory: Puritan Radicalism in New England, 1620–1660* (Middletown: Wesleyan University Press, 1984), 173.

44. Hall, ed., *Antinomian Controversy*, 262.

45. Hosmer, ed., *Winthrop's Journal*, 1:299, 195.

46. Hambrick-Stowe in *The Practice of Piety*, 80 and William K. B. Stoever in *'A Faire and Easie Way to Heaven': Covenant Theology and Antinomianism in Early Massachusetts* (Middletown: Wesleyan University Press, 1978) show that the orthodox New England clergy never held that works could influence the coming of grace. Stoever identifies the issue of sanctification as central to the Antinomian Controversy. David D. Hall in "On Common Ground: The Coherence of American Puritan Studies," in *The William and Mary Quarterly*, 3d series, vol. 44, no. 2 (April 1987), 199–213, presents an invaluable overview of current scholarship on the theological issues of the controversy.

47. Hall, ed., *Antinomian Controversy*, 246.

48. Ibid., 210.

49. Hosmer, ed., *Winthrop's Journal*, 209.

50. Ibid., 211.

51. Ibid., 212.

52. Ibid., 215.

53. Hall, ed., *Antinomian Controversy*, 220, 233–34, 238.

54. "The Examination of Mrs. Ann Hutchinson at the court at Newtown" in ibid., 312–48. All subsequent references to this document will appear by page number in the text.

55. Ibid., 263.

56. The experience of direct communication with God was frequently described in Puritan spiritual writing, as Patricia Caldwell points out in "The Antinomian Language Controversy," *The Harvard Theological Review* 69, no. 3–4 (July–Oct., 1976), 350. Andrew Delbanco holds that it was in New England that the practice became blasphemy, *Puritan Ordeal*, 135–37.

57. "A Report of the Trial of Mrs. Ann Hutchinson before the Church in Boston, March, 1638," in Hall, ed., *Antinomian Controversy*, 350–88. All subsequent references to this document will appear by page number in the text.

58. J. F. Maclear examines these issues in his "Anne Hutchinson and the Mortalist Heresy," *The New England Quarterly* 54, no. 1 (March 1981): 74–103.

59. For two discussions of language in the Hutchinson trials, see Patricia

Caldwell, "Antinomian Language Controversy," 345–67, and Lad Tobin, "A Radically Different Voice: Gender and Language in the Trials of Anne Hutchinson," *Early American Literature* 25, no. 3 (1990): 253–67.

60. Hall, ed., *Antinomian Controversy*, 218.

61. Hosmer, ed., *Winthrop's Journal*, 1:219.

62. See Hall, *Faithful Shepherd*, 94–117.

63. John Cotton, "Mr. Cotton's Rejoynder," in Hall ed., *Antinomian Controversy*, 107. Quoted in Stoever, *Faire and Easie Way*, 56. Stoever holds that the crucial disagreement in the Antinomian Controversy was over the relationship of faith, justification, and sanctification rather than over the necessity of preparation for salvation as Pettit maintains (see *Heart Prepared*, chap. 5).

64. Williston Walker, ed., *The Creeds and Platforms of Congregationalism* (New York: Charles Scribner's Sons, 1893; reprint Boston: Pilgrim Press, 1960), 205, 223.

65. See Gura, *Glimpse of Sion's Glory*, 162–64. For a different view, see Foster, *Long Argument*, 163.

Chapter 2

1. Haller, *Rise of Puritanism*, chap. 1, especially 27ff.

2. Thomas Hooker, *The Soul's Preparation for Christ: or a Treatise of Contrition*, 7th ed. (London, 1658), 247. Quoted in George Huntston Williams, "Essay I, The Life of Thomas Hooker in England and Holland, 1586–1633," in Williams, Pettit, et al., *Thomas Hooker: Writings*, 28.

3. Perry Miller and Thomas H. Johnson, eds., *The Puritans* (New York: American Book Company, 1938), 800. Quoted in Sargent Bush, Jr., *The Writings of Thomas Hooker: Spiritual Adventure in Two Worlds* (Madison: University of Wisconsin Press, 1980), 147.

4. Thomas Fuller, *History of the University of Cambridge and of Waltham Abbey with the Appeal of Injured Innocence* (London: Thomas Tegg, 1840), 207. Quoted in Haller, *Rise of Puritanism*, 20.

5. Lawrence Chaderton, quoted in E. S. Shuckburgh, *Emmanuel College* (London: T. E. Robinson and Co., 1909), 24–25. No source cited.

6. Baker MSS VI, 85–86. Quoted in James Bass Mullinger, *The University of Cambridge from the Royal Injunctions of 1535 to the Accession of Charles the First* (Cambridge: Cambridge University Press, 1884), 314.

7. Charles Henry Cooper, *Annals of Cambridge* (Cambridge: Warwick and Co., 1845), 3:280. Quoted in William T. Costello, S.J., *The Scholastic*

Curriculum at Early Seventeenth-Century Cambridge (Cambridge: Harvard University Press, 1958), 125.

8. J. A. W. Bennett and H. R. Trevor-Roper, eds., *Poems of Richard Corbett* (Oxford: Clarendon Press, 1955), 57.

9. George Huntston Williams, "Called by Thy Name, Leave Us Not: The Case of Mrs. Joan Drake, a Formative Episode in the Pastoral Career of Thomas Hooker in England," *Harvard Library Bulletin* 16, no. 2 (April 1968): 111–28, and no. 3 (July 1968): 278–303.

10. Mather, *Magnalia*, 1:303.

11. Haller, *Rise of Puritanism*, 56.

12. Anon., *The Firebrand Taken Out of the Fire, ore the Wonderful History, Case, and Cure of Mis(tress) Drake Sometimes the Wife of Francis Drake of Esher in the County of Surrey Esq; etc.* (London, 1654), 7. Quoted in Williams, "Called by Thy Name," 116. Williams shows the anonymous author to have been Jasper Heartwell (no. 3, 278–303).

13. Ibid., 24–25. Quoted in Williams, "Called by Thy Name," 117.

14. Thomas Hooker, *Poor Doubting Christian Drawn unto Christ* (Boston, 1743), 10. Quoted in Williams, "Called by Thy Name," 291. See also Amanda Porterfield, *Female Piety in Puritan New England: The Emergence of Religious Humanism* (New York: Oxford University Press, 1992), 48–49.

15. D. Lupton, *London and the Countrey Carbonadoed and Quartered into Seuerall Characters* (London, 1632), 125. Quoted in Ola Elizabeth Winslow, *Master Roger Williams, a Biography* (New York: Macmillan Co., 1957), 81.

16. Mather, *Magnalia*, 1:307.

17. Ibid., 313.

18. Charles Severn, M.D., ed., *Diary of the Rev. John Ward* (London: Henry Colburn, 1839), 131.

19. Mather, *Magnalia*, 1:314–15.

20. Thomas Hooker, *The Paterne of Perfection* (London, 1640), 4. Quoted in Bush, *Writings of Thomas Hooker: Spiritual Adventure*, 131.

21. Thomas Hooker, "The Faithful Covenanter," in Williams, Pettit, et al., *Thomas Hooker: Writings*, 209. Quoted in Norman Pettit, "Essay 2, The Order of Salvation in Thomas Hooker's Thought," in Williams, Pettit, et al., *Thomas Hooker: Writings*, 133.

22. Thomas Hooker, *The Soul's Implantation* (London, 1637), 178. Quoted in Pettit, *Heart Prepared*, 99.

23. Hooker, "Soul's Preparation," 248 ff. Quoted in Williams, "Essay I," Williams, Pettit, et al., *Thomas Hooker: Writings*, 29.

24. John Eliot, Letter III, transcribed F. J. Powicke, "Some Unpublished Correspondence of. . . Richard Baxter and. . . Eliot," *Bulletin of the John Rylands Library* 15, no. 2 (July 1931). Quoted in Williams, "Essay I," Williams, Pettit, et al., *Thomas Hooker: Writings*, 21–22.

25. Mather, *Magnalia*, 1:305.

26. John Fuller, "To the Reader," in John Beadle, *The Diary of a Thankful Christian* (London: Thomas Parkhurst, 1656), 2–3.

27. *Calendar of State Papers Domestic, Charles I, 1629–1631*, 142, no. 113 (hereafter abbreviated as *CSPD, C I*). Quoted in Harold Smith, *The Ecclesiastical History of Essex* (Colcester: Benham and Co., 1932), 33.

28. McGiffert, ed., *God's Plot*, 39. All subsequent references to Shepard's *Autobiography* and *Journal* appear by page number in the text.

29. Will of John Shepard of Foscote, May 7, 1619, Northamptonshire Record Office, Delapre Abbey, Northamptonshire, P113. Although unverified, from internal evidence and from Thomas Shepard's own account, this document appears to be the will of his grandfather, William Shepard of Towcester, April 25, 1617, Northamptonshire Record Office, P57.

30. List of Feoffees for the Sponne Charity, 1566–1834, Northamptonshire Record Office, TC793.

31. Alan Crossley, ed., *A History of the County of Oxford*, vol. X of *Victoria History of the Counties of England* (Oxford: Oxford University Press, 1972), 98.

32. Quoted in P. M. Rattansi, "The Scientific Background," in C. A. Patrides and Raymond B. Waddington, eds., *The Age of Milton: Backgrounds to Seventeenth Century Literature* (Manchester: Manchester University Press, 1980), 216, 221.

33. John Aubrey, "Thomas Hobbes," in Andrew Clark, ed., *"Brief Lives," Chiefly of Contemporaries, Set Down by John Aubrey, between the Years 1669 and 1696* (Oxford: Oxford University Press, 1898), 132, 133.

34. William Drummond, "A Cypresse Grove," in L. E. Kastner, ed., *Poetical Works of William Drummond of Hawthornden with 'A Cypresse Grove* (Manchester: Manchester University Press, 1913), 2:78. Quoted in Christopher Hill, *Intellectual Origins of the English Revolution* (Oxford: Oxford University Press, 1965), 8.

35. John Preston, "To the Reader," *Sermons Preached before His Maiestie; and upon Other Special Occasions* (London: Leonard Greene, 1630), 44–45. Quoted in Haller, *Rise of Puritanism*, 167.

36. See pp. 29–30.

37. See McGiffert, "Thomas Shepard: The Practice of Piety," *God's Plot*, 28; and Pettit, *Heart Prepared*, 107.

38. William H. D. Longstaffe, ed., *The Acts of the High Commission Court within the Diocese of Durham*, Surtees Society, *Publications*, 34 (Durham, 1858), 9.

39. Ibid., 9.

40. Thomas Shepard, *The Sincere Convert: Discovering The small number of true believers, And the great difficulty of Saving Conversion*, 4th ed., in *Works*, 1:95.

41. Ibid., 8.

42. Ibid., 13.

43. Ibid., 18.

44. Ibid., 20

45. Ibid., 28.

46. Ibid., 43.

47. Ibid., 45, 49.

48. Ibid., 50.

49. Ibid., 62.

50. See Michael Walzer, *The Revolution of the Saints: A Study in the Origins of Radical Politics* (Cambridge: Harvard University Press, 1965), especially chaps. 1 and 2.

51. See Thomas Werge, *Thomas Shepard* (Boston: Twayne Publishers, 1987), chap. 4, for a discussion of the contrasting moods and methods of *The Sincere Convert* and *The Sound Believer*.

CHAPTER 3

1. Mather, *Magnalia*, 1:304.

2. *CSPD, C I*, 142, no. 113. Quoted in Smith, *Ecclesiastical History*, 33–34.

3. *CSPD, C I*, 144, no. 36, in T. W. Davids, *Annals of Evangelical Nonconformity in the County of Essex* (London: Jackson, Walford and Hodder, 1863), 152.

4. *CSPD, C I*, 142, no. 113, ibid., 151.

5. See Williams, "Essay I," in Williams, Pettit, et al., *Thomas Hooker: Writings*, 17, for a description of the meeting.

6. *CSPD, C I*, 151, no. 37, in Davids, *Annals*, 152–53.

7. Thomas Hooker, "The Danger of Desertion" (ca. April 1631), in Williams, Pettit, et al., *Thomas Hooker: Writings*, 244–46.

8. Mather, *Magnalia*, 1:307.

9. Ibid., 308.

10. Thomas Hooker, "Letter to John Cotton from Rotterdam" (ca. April 1633), in Williams, Pettit et al., *Thomas Hooker: Writings*, 297–98.

11. Hosmer, ed., *Winthrop's Journal*, 1:90.

12. Thomas Prince, *A Chronological History of New England in the Form of Annals*, new ed. (Boston: Cummings, Hilliard and Co., 1826), 412.

13. Mather, *Magnalia*, 1:393.

14. Ibid., 309.

15. Hosmer, ed., *Winthrop's Journal*, 1:111.

16. Shepard, *Sincere Convert*, in *Works*, 1:iii.

17. See page 14.

18. Essex Record Office, Chelmsford, Essex, Documents D/ACA47 11V and D/ACV 92V.

19. Prince, *Annals*, 338–39.

20. Henry Jessey, "Letter to John Winthrop, Jr., January 9, 1631–2" in *The Winthrop Papers* (Massachusetts Historical Society, Boston, 1943), 3:59. Laud's second triennial visitation to Essex began on August 30, 1631. On September 3, he held Court at Kelvedon. Shepard's reference to the occasion was read by McGiffert (*God's Plot*, 52) as Reldon or Peldon instead of Keldon, which was a frequent contraction of Kelvedon [see Philip Morant, *History and Antiquities of the County of Essex* (London: T. Osborn, 1768), 2:150; and Davids, *Annals*, 302].

21. R. H., "To the Christian Reader" in Thomas Shepard, *Four Necessary Cases of Conscience of Daily Use* (London, date illegible), B3–B4. "R. H." can be positively identified as Richard Harlakenden of Earles Colne, older brother of Shepard's friend, Roger, by biographical information in the dedication "to his dear and only son, R. H.," the only child "of a precious saint once on earth . . . thy life was some cause of her death," A4. The marriage of Richard Harlakenden to Alice Mildmay, her death at the time of the birth of the younger Richard, and the three years elapsing before his remarriage are noted in the unpublished "Account Book" of three generations of Harlakendens: Roger, Richard (father), and Richard (son), and in the unpublished Earles Colne Parish Register, both in the Essex County Record Office.

CHAPTER 4

1. Hosmer, ed., *Winthrop's Journal*, 1:124, 128.

2. Ibid., 132.

3. Edward Johnson, *The Wonder-Working Providence of Sion's Savior in New England* (1654), ed. J. Franklin Jamison (New York: C. Scribner's Son, 1910), 106.

4. "The Rev. Robert Stansby to John Wilson" (April 17, 1637), in *Massachusetts Historical Society Collections*, series IV, 5 (Cambridge, 1865), 10–11; and William Hubbard, *A General History of New England* (Boston: C. C. Little and J. Brown, 1848), 173. Quoted in Pettit, *Heart Prepared*, 90–91.

5. "Stansby to Wilson," *Massachusetts Historical Society Collections*, series IV, 5, 11. See also Gura, *Glimpse of Sion's Glory*, 165–66; and Delbanco, *Puritan Ordeal*, 180–81.

6. See Frank Charles Shuffleton, *Thomas Hooker, 1586–1647* (Princeton: Princeton University Press, 1977), 195–96.

7. There were no Hooker publications for the years 1634–1636. See Sargent Bush, Jr., "A Bibliography of the Published Writings of Thomas Hooker" in Williams, Pettit et al., *Thomas Hooker: Writings*, 397–400.

8. See George Selement and Bruce C. Woolley, eds., *Thomas Shepard's "Confessions": Collections of the Colonial Society of Massachusetts* 58 (Boston: The Society, 1981): 93, 110, 147, for background information about William Manning, William Andrews, and Jane Wilkinson Winship—all of whom were part of Hooker's flock as well as Shepard's. Manning and Andrews were full members under Hooker; Winship may have been simply part of the congregation. The question of the nature of the continuity between Hooker's and Shepard's churches remained unresolved for many years in Cambridge. Abiel Holmes, pastor 1792–1831, held that "Mr. S. was properly the first minister of the first church now in Cambridge" (Stephen Paschall Sharples, ed., *Records of the Church of Christ at Cambridge in New England, 1632–1830* (Boston: E. Putnam, 1906), 286. Finally, on the occasion of their tercentennial, the two successor parish churches in Cambridge—the First Church in Cambridge, Unitarian Universalist and the First Church in Cambridge, Congregational, United Church of Christ—agreed to list both 1633 and 1636 as dates for their founding. The First Church of Christ (Center Church) in Hartford claims 1632 for its founding because of the initial gathering of the church on that date (see text, p. 76). All of these dates were certainly founding moments for the three congregations.

9. Thomas Shepard, *Theses Sabbaticae, Or, the Doctrine of the Sabbath* in *Works* (1649), 3:25.

10. The two descendants of the First Church in Cambridge that emerged in 1829 as separate Unitarian and Congregational churches remain gathered

churches. At the moment of admission to both churches, new members affirm their commitment to a covenant.

11. See page 27, note 38.

12. Shepard, *Ten Virgins*, in *Works*, 2:41–42.

13. Shepard, *Sincere Convert*, in *Works*, 1:8; *Ten Virgins*, in *Works*, 2:48. See Porterfield, *Female Piety*, 55–56.

14. Shepard, *Sound Believer*, in *Works*, 1:140. For a discussion of this aspect of Shepard's thought, see Pettit, *Heart Prepared*, 109.

15. See page 64. Shepard, *Sound Believer*, in *Works*, 1:146.

16. See page 21.

17. Thomas Shepard and John Allin, *A Defense of the Answer Made unto the Nine Questions or Positions Sent from New-England against the Reply Thereto by... John Ball* (London: R. Cotes for Andrew Crooke, 1648), 194.

18. "Thomas Shepard to Richard Mather" (April 2, 1635). Quoted in John A. Albro, *The Life of Thomas Shepard* (Boston: Massachusetts Sabbath School Society, 1847), 214, 216.

19. Fifty-one confessions from a notebook at the New England Historic Genealogical Society in Boston were transcribed and edited by Selement and Woolley as Thomas Shepard's "Confessions" (see above, n. 8). Mary Rhinelander McCarl found sixteen more among the Mather papers in the American Antiquarian Society in Worcester, Massachusetts; they were transcribed and edited by her and published as "Thomas Shepard's Record of Relations of Religious Experience, 1648–1649," in *The William and Mary Quarterly*, 3d ser., vol. 48, no. 3, 432–66. Thirty-three confessions selected from both collections are included in McGiffert's *God's Plot* with an accompanying analysis.

20. Shepard, *Ten Virgins*, in *Works*, 2:188.

21. Shepard, *Defense of the Answer*, 189.

22. Shepard, *Ten Virgins*, in *Works*, 2:631; and *Sound Believer*, ibid., 1:153. See Patricia Caldwell, *The Puritan Conversion Narrative: the Beginnings of American Expression* (Cambridge: Cambridge University Press, 1983), especially 144–50, for an analysis of Shepard's attitude about public confession.

23. The italics are mine.

24. Sharples, "List of Members in the Church of Cambridge, 1658–1667, in the Handwriting of Rev. Mr. Jonathan Mitchel," *Records*, 21. McCarl, "Shepard's Record of Relations," 436–37, 450–51.

25. Shepard, *Ten Virgins*, in *Works*, 2:633.

26. Ibid., 26, 375 ff.

27. Thomas Shepard, *Wine for Gospel Wantons: or, Cautions against Spirituall Drunkenness*, Sermon, June 25, 1645 (Cambridge, 1661).

28. See page 65.

29. "Thomas Shepard to John Cotton," in Hall, *Antinomian Controversy*, 25–29.

30. Shepard, *Ten Virgins*, in *Works*, 2:23.

31. Ibid., 133–34.

32. Thomas Shepard, *New England's Lamentation for Old England's Present Errors* (London, 1645), 4 . See Stoever, *Faire and Easie Way*, 180–83, for a discussion of the ambiguities of orthodox Puritanism.

33. Walker, ed., *Creeds and Platforms*, 185–86.

34. Shepard, *The Saint's Jewel, Showing How to Apply the Promise*, in *Works*, 1:292, 288.

35. Shepard, *Subjection to Christ, in all his Ordinances and Appointments, The best means to preserve our Liberty*, in *Works*, 3:310.

36. Shepard, *Sound Believer*, in *Works*, 1:210. See Hambrick-Stowe, *Practice of Piety*, 76–85, for a discussion of the cycle of conversion and reconversion in Puritan thought and worship.

37. For a discussion of anxiety and assurance in Shepard's life and thought, see McGiffert, "Thomas Shepard: The Practice of Piety," *God's Plot*, 24–26; and Stoever, *Faire and Easie Way*, 148–50 and 229–30, note 32.

38. Shepard, *The Saints Jewel*, in *Works*, 1:289.

39. John Coolidge, *The Pauline Renaissance in England: Puritanism and the Bible* (Oxford: Clarendon Press, 1970), 147.

40. Shepard, *Subjection to Christ*, in *Works*, 3:326.

41. Shepard, *Ten Virgins*, in *Works*, 2:45.

42. Ibid., 189.

43. Ibid., 380–83.

44. Shepard, *Subjection to Christ*, in *Works*, 3:327–29.

45. Shepard, *Ten Virgins*, in *Works*, 2:65.

46. Johnson, *Wonder-Working Providence*, 108, 107.

47. Mather, *Magnalia*, 2:75.

48. Giles Fermin, *The Real Christian or a Treatise of Effectual Calling* (London: Dorman Newman, 1670), 3, 55.

49. Hambrick-Stowe, *Practice of Piety*, 88–90.

50. Selement and Woolley, *Shepard's "Confessions,"* 131; and Caldwell, *Puritan Conversion Narrative*, 135.

51. Nathaniel B. Shurtleff, ed., *Records of the Governor and Company of the Massachusetts Bay in New England* (Boston: William White, 1853), 1:217; Johnson, *Wonder-Working Providence*, 201.

52. In his *A Treatise Concerning Religious Affections*, Edwards quotes Shepard more than any other single author, as John A. Albro pointed out in his *Life of Thomas Shepard*, 318–19. He was especially influenced by Shepard's descriptions of the conversion process and his clear distinction between true sincerity and hypocrisy. See also "Editor's Introduction" to John E. Smith, ed., *Jonathan Edwards Religious Affections* (New Haven: Yale University Press, 1959), 53–57; and Werge, *Thomas Shepard*, 99–102.

53. McKenzie, *Lectures*, 198.

54. Although most recent scholars cite Albro as the editor of the 1853 edition of the *Works of Thomas Shepard*, I have been unable to find evidence confirming his editorship. I am grateful to Harold C. Worthley, Director of the Congregational Library, Boston, for the following information, which brings Albro's role as editor into serious question. The 1852 Annual Report of the Doctrinal Tract and Book Society, publishers of the edition, refers to its forthcoming publication but does not mention Albro; nor does he appear among the listed life members and officers of the society. In addition, the "Advertisement," which introduces the first volume of the edition refers to Albro in the third person as the author of the "Life of Thomas Shepard," which is included in the first volume, and is signed simply by "The Editor." Nowhere is Albro mentioned as editor.

55. Mather, *Magnalia*, 1:352.

56. Richard Baxter, *A Christian Directory: Or, A Summ of Practical Theologie, and Cases of Conscience* (London: Robert White for Nevil Simmons, 1673), 480. Quoted in Joyce L. Irwin, *Womanhood in Radical Protestantism, 1525–1675* (New York: Edwin Mellen Press, 1979), 112.

57. Mary Astell, *Some Reflections Upon Marriage*, 4th ed., (London, 1730), 99. Quoted in Natalie Zeman Davis, *Society and Culture in Early Modern France* (Stanford: Stanford University Press, 1975), 142. Porterfield points out that Anne Hutchinson also accepted without question the patriarchal society of which she was a part and drew her authority partly from her submission to it. See *Female Piety*, 100–101, 106.

58. Lord Chief Baron Hale (1663), quoted in Margaret J. M. Ezell, *The Patriarch's Wife: Literary Evidence and the History of the Family* (Chapel Hill: University of North Carolina Press, 1987), 128.

59. *The Lawes Resolutions of Womens Rights: Or, the Lawes Provision for*

Women (London, 1632). Quoted in Roger Thompson, *Women in Stuart England and America, a Comparative Study* (London: Routledge and Kegan Paul, Ltd., 1974), 162.

60. Agrippa von Nettesheim, Henry Cornelius, *Female Pre-eminence: Or the Dignity and Excellency of That Sex, above the Male,* trans. Henry Care (1670), 1. Quoted in Ezell, *Patriarch's Wife,* 57.

61. Anne Bradstreet, "Prologue," in Jeannine Hensley, ed., *Works of Anne Bradstreet* (Cambridge: The Belknap Press of Harvard University Press, 1967), 16.

62. For insights into the ambiguities in the lives of seventeenth-century women, I am very much indebted to conversations with Anne Ferry, to her "Milton's Creation of Eve" in *Studies in English Literature 1500–1900* 28, no. 1, 113–32, and to Ezell, *Patriarch's Wife,* especially chap. 1, 9–35.

63. For a discussion of sixteenth-century Church of England, Roman Catholic, and Puritan marriage doctrine, see James Turner Johnson, *A Society Ordained by God: English Puritan Marriage Doctrine in the First Half of the Seventeenth Century* (Nashville: Abingdon Press, 1970), 19–23, 38–49.

64. Thomas Gataker, *A Good Wife Gods Gift* (London, 1623). Cited in Johnson, *Society Ordained by God,* 22.

65. William and Malleville Haller, "The Puritan Art of Love," *Huntington Library Quarterly* 5, no. 2 (January 1942): 154.

66. Benjamin Wadsworth, *The Well-Ordered Family* (Boston: Nicholas Buttolph, 1712), 36. Quoted in Edmond S. Morgan, *The Puritan Family: Religion and Domestic Relations in Seventeenth Century New England,* new ed. (New York: Harper and Row, 1966), 48.

67. See Laurel Thatcher Ulrich, *Goodwives: Image and Reality in the Lives of Women in Northern New England, 1650–1750* (New York: Alfred A. Knopf, 1982), Part I, 11–86.

68. See Porterfield, *Female Piety,* 87–115.

69. Mary Maples Dunn shows a degree of participation by women in church meetings in John Fiske's church in Wenham before 1655, "Saints and Sisters," in Janet Wilson James, ed., *Women in American Religion* (Philadelphia: University of Pennsylvania Press, 1980), 34–35.

70. Walker, ed., *Creeds and Platforms,* 210.

71. Ibid., 214.

72. John Winthrop, "A Short Story of the Rise, Reign, and Ruine of the Antinomians, Familists, and Libertines," in Hall, ed., *Antinomian Controversy,* 205–6.

73. Hall, ed., *Antinomian Controversy*, 365.

74. Hambrick-Stowe, *Practice of Piety*, 43. Lad Tobin, following the thesis of Carol Gilligan in *In a Different Voice: Psychological Theory and Women's Development* (Cambridge: Harvard University Press, 1982), holds that the attraction of Hutchinson to spirit religion and the language she uses are related to the importance of intimacy in personal relations in her own life as a woman. See "A Radically Different Voice: Gender and Language in the Trials of Anne Hutchinson," *Early American Literature* 25, no. 3 (1990), 256–58.

75. See page 94.

76. Shepard was married three times: to Margaret Touteville (July 1632), Joanna Hooker (October 1637), and Margaret Boradel (September 1647). His *Autobiography* and *Journal* were concluded before his third marriage. Elsewhere in his papers, there are no descriptive references to Margaret Boradel, to whom he was married for less than two years before his death on August 25, 1649.

77. Shepard, *The Church Membership of Children, and their Right to Baptism*, in *Works*, 3:530.

78. Shepard, *Sound Believer*, in *Works*, 1:241.

79. Shepard, *Ten Virgins*, in *Works*, 2:47–49.

80. Thomas Hooker and Susannah Garbrand were married on April 3, 1621. See Williams, "Essay I" in Williams, Pettit, et al., *Thomas Hooker: Writings*, 5.

81. See page 112.

82. Shepard, mss. Quoted in Cotton Mather, *The Temple Opening* (Boston: S. Phillips, 1709), 30–31.

83. The confession of Goodwife Jackson in McCarl's collection was recorded by a hand other than Shepard's but sewn into the group recorded by him. See McCarl, "Shepard's Record of Relations," 433.

84. McCarl ed., "Shepard's Record of Relations," 433–34.

85. Selement and Woolley, eds., *Shepard's "Confessions,"* 81, 130, 139. All subsequent references are identified by page number in the text. McCarl, ed., "Shepard's Record of Relations," 435.

86. See especially, Mary Maples Dunn, "Saints and Sisters," 27–46; Gerald F. Moran, "'Sisters' in Christ: Women and the Church in Seventeenth-Century New England," 47–65; and Laural Thatcher Ulrich, "Vertuous Women Found: New England Ministerial Literature, 1668–1735", 67–87— all in James, ed., *Women in American Religion*; Martha Tomhave Blaufelt and

Rosemary Skinner Keller, "Women and Revivalism: The Puritan and Wesleyan Traditions," in Rosemary Radford Ruether and Rosemary Skinner Keller, eds., *Women and Religion in America*, vol. II: *The Colonial and Revolutionary Periods* (San Francisco: Harper and Row, 1983), 316–28; Ann Douglas, *The Feminization of American Culture* (New York: Alfred A. Knopf, 1977), especially Introduction and chap. 2; and Porterfield, *Female Piety*, 9.

87. Laurel Thatcher Ulrich, "Vertuous Women," in James, ed., *Women in American Religion*, 75. See also Cohen, *God's Caress*, 223.

88. Hall, *Worlds of Wonder*, 23–25, 32.

89. See Caldwell, *Puritan Conversion Narrative*, 183–86.

90. Kathleen M. Swaim cites other women's texts and points out that Shepard's sermons on the parable of the Ten Virgins influenced female confessors in the earlier group of narratives edited by Selement and Woolley far more than their male counterparts, who mention the text much less frequently. See her "'Come and Hear': Women's Puritan Evidences," in Margo Culley, ed., *American Women's Autobiography: Fea(s)ts of Memory* (Madison: University of Wisconsin Press, 1992), 43–44. There are no references to the text in the later group of confessions edited by McCarl, presumably because the series of sermons concluded in May of 1640.

91. See Anne Ferry, *The Inward Language: Sonnets of Wyatt, Sidney, Shakespeare, Donne* (Chicago and London: University of Chicago Press, 1983), 40–41 for a discussion of "the imperative to know thyself" in its sixteenth-century context.

92. Caldwell, *Puritan Conversion Narrative*, 40–41.

93. See appendix for biographical information.

94. McCarl, ed., "Shepard's Record of Relations," 460.

95. There are many examples among the male narratives of experiences of shame and consequent unwillingness to speak, but none that relate to their wives. Cohen, in *God's Caress*, 151, n. 49, cites some of these references.

96. Rosamond R. Rosenmeier, "Divine Translation: A Contribution to the Study of Anne Bradstreet's Method in the Marriage Poems," *Early American Literature* 12, no. 2, 125.

97. Ulrich, *Goodwives*, 216. See also Porterfield, *Female Piety*, 14.

98. McCarl, ed., "Shepard's Record of Relations," 464.

99. See pp. 64–65, 93–94, 105–6.

100. See Selement and Woolley, eds., Shepard's *"Confessions,"* 121, 131, 191, for other examples of this kind of humiliation. The use of explicit language of submission occurs in fourteen of the women's confessions.

101. McCarl, ed., "Thomas Shepard's Record of Relations," 454, 457.

102. Ibid., 466.

103. Cotton Mather, "Tabitha Rediviva," in Ruether and Keller, *Women and Religion*, 2:339.

104. Hensley, ed., *Works of Anne Bradstreet*, 235–37, 241; Hall, ed., *Antinomian Controversy*, 412.

105. Caldwell, *Puritan Conversion Narrative*, 26.

106. George Huntston Williams, *The Radical Reformation*, 3d ed., vol. 15: *Sixteenth Century Essays and Studies*, ed. Charles G. Nauert, Jr. (Kirksville, Mo.: Sixteenth Century Journal Publishers, 1992), 762.

107. See especially Douglas, *Feminization of American Culture*, 5–13 and chaps. 1–5.

EPILOGUE

1. See Perry Miller, *The New England Mind: From Colony to Province* (Cambridge: Harvard University Press, 1953), book I; Morgan, *Visible Saints*, chap. 4; Emory Elliott, *Power and the Pulpit in Colonial New England* (Princeton: Princeton University Press, 1975), chaps. 1 and 2; and Foster, *Long Argument*, chap. 5.

2. Shepard, *Church Membership of Children*, in *Works*, 3:540, 536–37.

3. Jonathan Mitchel and Richard Mather, "Answer to the Apologetical Preface," in *A Defense of the Answer and Arguments of the Synod met at Boston in the Year 1662* (Cambridge: Hezekiah Usher, 1664), 45.

4. Walker, ed., *Creeds and Platforms*, 325, 327, 328.

5. Sharples, ed., *Records*, 76. There is no mention of the use of the new covenant in Mitchel's surviving records, which consist only of a list of church members. The covenant text first appears in the papers of William Brattle (pastor 1696–1717) but was almost certainly in use, at least in some form, in Mitchel's time. I have not been able to find evidence in the church records to substantiate clearly Alexander McKenzie's assertion that the covenant was still in use in the pastorate of Abiel Holmes through 1828, "although during the later years but few persons availed themselves of its provisions." Included in Holmes's records is a list headed "Renewal of Covenant for the Baptism of children," which is distinct from the list of "Admissions to Full Communion." Possibly it is a continuation of the old Half-Way Covenant form. See Sharples, *Records*, 455–68, and McKenzie, *Lectures*, 112.

6. Ibid., 76.

7. Article XI of the By-Laws as amended on March 28, 1993, the First

Church in Cambridge, Unitarian Universalist. I am indebted to C. Conrad Wright for helpful advice and for sharing with me his knowledge of the history of the First Church in Cambridge, Unitarian Universalist.

8. Covenant Testimony and Covenant of the First Church in Cambridge, Congregational, United Church of Christ.

Selected Bibliography

Primary Sources

Bradstreet, Anne. *Works of Anne Bradstreet*, edited by Jeannine Hensley. Cambridge: The Belknap Press of Harvard University Press, 1967.

Cotton, John. *John Cotton on the Churches of New England*, edited by Larzer Ziff. Cambridge: The Belknap Press of Harvard University Press, 1968.

Fermin, Giles. *The Real Christian or a Treatise of Effectual Calling*. London: Dorman Newman, 1670.

Fuller, Thomas. *History of the Worthies of England* (1662), edited by John Freeman. London: Allen and Unwin, 1952.

Hall, David D., ed. *The Antinomian Controversy, 1636–1638: A Documentary History*. 2d ed. Durham and London: Duke University Press, 1990.

Hooker, Thomas. *Thomas Hooker: Writings in England and Holland, 1626–1633*, edited by George H. Williams, Norman Pettit, Winfried Herget, and Sargent Bush, Jr. Cambridge: Harvard University Press, 1975.

Johnson, Edward. *The Wonder-Working Providence of Sion's Savior in New England* (1654), edited by J. Franklin Jamison. New York: C. Scribner's Son, 1910.

Laud, William. *The Autobiography of Dr. William Laud*. Oxford: John Henry Parker, 1839.

———. *The History of the Troubles and Tryal of the Most Reverend Father in God, William Laud Archbishop of Canterbury* in *The Works of Archbishop Laud*. Vol. 3. Oxford: John Henry Parker, 1853.

Mather, Cotton. *Magnalia Christi Americana or the Ecclesiastical History of New England*. 2 vols. Hartford: Silas Andrus and Son, 1820.

———. *The Temple Opening*. Boston: S. Phillips, 1709.

Mitchel, Jonathan, and Richard Mather. *A Defense of the Answer and Argu-*

ments of the Synod met at Boston in the Year 1662. Cambridge: Hezekiah Usher, 1664.

Shepard, Thomas. *Autobiography.* In *God's Plot: The Paradoxes of Puritan Piety, Being the Autobiography and Journal of Thomas Shepard,* edited by Michael McGiffert. Amherst: University of Massachusetts Press, 1972.

———. *A Defense of the Answer Made unto the Nine Questions or Positions Sent from New-England against the Reply Thereto by John Ball.* With John Allin. London: Andrew Crooke, 1648.

———. *Journal.* In *God's Plot* (above).

———. *New England's Lamentation for Old England's Present Errors.* London, 1645.

———. *Thomas Shepard's Confessions,* Colonial Society of Massachusetts Collections, 58. Edited by George Selement and Bruce C. Woolley. Boston: The Society, 1981.

———. "Thomas Shepard's Record of Relations of Religious Experience, 1648–1649," edited by Mary Rhinelander McCarl. *The William and Mary Quarterly,* 3d ser., 48:432–66.

———. *Wine for Gospel Wantons: Or, Cautions against Spirituall Drunkenness.* Sermon, June 25, 1645. Cambridge, 1661.

———. *The Works of Thomas Shepard.* 3 vols. Boston: Doctrinal Tract and Book Society, 1853.

Walker, Williston, ed., *The Creeds and Platforms of Congregationalism.* New York: Charles Scribner's Sons, 1893. Reprint. Boston: Pilgrim Press, 1960.

Winthrop, John. *Winthrop's Journal, "History of New England, 1630–1649."* Edited by James Kendall Hosmer. 2 vols. New York: Barnes and Noble, Inc., 1946.

SECONDARY SOURCES

Albro, John A. *The Life of Thomas Shepard.* Boston: Massachusetts Sabbath School Society, 1847.

Bailyn, Bernard. *The New England Merchants in the Seventeenth Century.* Cambridge: Harvard University Press, 1955.

Bush, Sargent, Jr. "A Bibliography of the Published Writings of Thomas Hooker," 397–400. In *Thomas Hooker: Writings in England and Holland, 1626–1633,* edited by George H. Williams, Norman Pettit, Winfried Herget, and Sargent Bush, Jr. Cambridge: Harvard University Press, 1975.

————. *The Writings of Thomas Hooker: Spiritual Adventure in Two Worlds.* Madison: University of Wisconsin Press, 1980.

Caldwell, Patricia. "The Antinomian Language Controversy." *The Harvard Theological Review* 69 (July–Oct. 1976).

————. *The Puritan Conversion Narrative: the Beginnings of American Expression.* Cambridge: Cambridge University Press, 1983.

Cohen, Charles Lloyd. *God's Caress: The Psychology of Puritan Religious Experience.* Oxford: Oxford University Press, 1986.

Coolidge, John. *The Pauline Renaissance in England: Puritanism and the Bible.* Oxford: Clarendon Press, 1970.

Costello, William T., S.J., *The Scholastic Curriculum at Early Seventeenth-Century Cambridge.* Cambridge: Harvard University Press, 1958.

Davids, T. W. *Annals of Evangelical Non-conformity in the County of Essex.* London: Jackson, Walford and Hodder, 1863.

Davies, Horton. *The Worship of the English Puritans.* Westminster: Dacre Press, 1948.

Davis, Natalie Zeman. *Society and Culture in Early Modern France.* Stanford: Stanford University Press, 1975.

Delbanco, Andrew. *The Puritan Ordeal.* Cambridge: Harvard University Press, 1989.

————. "Thomas Shepard's America: The Biography of an Idea." In *Studies in Biography,* edited by Daniel Aaron, 159–82. Harvard English Studies 8. Cambridge: Harvard University Press, 1978.

Douglas, Ann. *The Feminization of American Culture.* New York: Alfred A. Knopf, 1977.

Dunn, Mary Maples. "Saints and Sisters." In *Women in American Religion,* edited by Janet Wilson James. Philadelphia: University of Pennsylvania Press, 1980.

Elliott, Emory. *Power and the Pulpit in Colonial New England.* Princeton: Princeton University Press, 1975.

Ezell, Margaret J. M. *The Patriarch's Wife: Literary Evidence and the History of the Family.* Chapel Hill: University of North Carolina Press, 1987.

Ferry, Anne. "Milton's Creation of Eve." *Studies in English Literature 1500–1900,* 28: 113–32.

Foster, Stephen. *The Long Argument: English Puritanism and the Shaping of New England Culture, 1570–1700.* Chapel Hill and London: University of North Carolina Press, 1991.

Gura, Philip F. *A Glimpse of Sion's Glory: Puritan Radicalism in New England,*

1620–1660. Middletown, Conn.: Wesleyan University Press, 1984.

Hall, David D. "On Common Ground: The Coherence of American Puritan Studies," in *The William and Mary Quarterly*, 3d ser., 44 (April 1987): 199–213.

———. *The Faithful Shepherd: A History of the New England Ministry in the Seventeenth Century.* Chapel Hill: University of North Carolina Press, 1972.

———. "Understanding the Puritans." In *Colonial America: Essays in Politics and Social Development,* edited by Stanley N. Katz. Boston: Little Brown and Co., 1971.

———. *Worlds of Wonder, Days of Judgment: Popular Religious Belief in Early New England.* New York: Alfred A. Knopf, 1989.

Haller, William. *The Rise of Puritanism, or, the Way to the New Jerusalem as Set Forth in Pulpit and Press from Thomas Cartwright to John Liliburne and John Milton, 1570–1643.* New York: Columbia University Press, 1938.

Haller, William, and Malleville Haller. "The Puritan Art of Love." *Huntington Library Quarterly* 5:154.

Hambrick-Stowe, Charles E. *The Practice of Piety: Puritan Devotional Disciplines in Seventeenth Century New England.* Chapel Hill: University of North Carolina Press, 1982.

Hill, Christopher. *Intellectual Origins of the English Revolution.* Oxford: Oxford University Press, 1965.

———. *Society and Puritanism in Pre-Revolutionary England,* 2d ed. New York: Schocken Books, 1967.

———. *The Collected Essays of Christopher Hill.* 3 vols. Amherst: University of Massachusetts Press, 1986.

Irwin, Joyce L. *Womanhood in Radical Protestantism, 1525–1675.* New York: Edwin Mellen Press, 1979.

Johnson, James Turner. *A Society Ordained by God: English Puritan Marriage Doctrine in the First Half of the Seventeenth Century.* Nashville: Abingdon Press, 1970.

Maclear, J. F. "Anne Hutchinson and the Mortalist Heresy." *The New England Quarterly* 54 (March 1981): 74–103.

McGiffert, Michael. "Grace and Works: The Rise and Division of Covenant Divinity in Elizabethan Puritanism." *Harvard Theological Review* 75 (1982): 463–502.

———. "The People Speak: Confessions of Lay Men and Women." In *God's Plot: Puritan Spirituality in Thomas Shepard's Cambridge,* edited by Michael McGiffert, 135–48. Revised and expanded edition. Amherst: University of Massachusetts Press, 1994.

———. "Thomas Shepard: The Practice of Piety." In *God's Plot* (above).

McKenzie, Alexander. *Lectures on the History of the First Church in Cambridge.* Boston: Congregational Publishing Society, 1873.

Miller, Perry. *Orthodoxy in Massachusetts, 1630–1650.* Cambridge: Harvard University Press, 1933.

———. *The New England Mind: The Seventeenth Century.* Cambridge: Harvard University Press, 1939.

———. *The New England Mind: From Colony to Province.* Cambridge: Harvard University Press, 1953.

Moran, Gerald F. "'Sisters' in Christ: Women and the Church in Seventeenth-Century New England." In *Women in American Religion,* edited by Janet Wilson James. Philadelphia: University of Pennsylvania Press, 1980.

Morant, Philip. *History and Antiquities of the County of Essex.* London: T. Osborn, 1768.

Morgan, Edmond S. *The Puritan Family: Religion and Domestic Relations in Seventeenth Century New England,* new ed. New York: Harper and Row, 1966.

———. *Visible Saints: The History of a Puritan Idea.* New York: New York University Press, 1963.

Morgan, Irvonwy. *The Godly Preachers of the Elizabethan Church.* London: Epworth Press, 1965.

Morison, Samuel Eliot. *Builders of the Bay Colony.* Boston: Houghton Mifflin Co., 1930.

Mullinger, James Bass. *The University of Cambridge from the Royal Injunctions of 1535 to the Accession of Charles the First.* Cambridge: Cambridge University Press, 1884.

Paige, Lucius R. *History of Cambridge, Massachusetts, 1630–1877.* Boston: H. O. Houghton and Co., 1877.

Pettit, Norman. "Essay 2: The Order of Salvation in Thomas Hooker's Thought." In *Thomas Hooker: Writings in England and Holland, 1586–1633,* edited by George H. Williams, Norman Pettit, Winfried Herget, and Sargent Bush, Jr. Cambridge: Harvard University Press, 1975.

———. *The Heart Prepared: Grace and Conversion in Puritan Spiritual Life.* Second ed. with a new Introduction by David D. Hall. Middletown, Conn.: Wesleyan University Press, 1989.

Porterfield, Amanda. *Female Piety in Puritan New England: The Emergence of Religious Humanism.* New York: Oxford University Press, 1992.

Rosenmeier, Rosamond R. "Divine Translation: A Contribution to the Study of Anne Bradstreet's Method in the Marriage Poems." *Early American Literature* 12:125.

Ruether, Rosemary Radford, and Rosemary Skinner Keller, eds. *Women and Religion in America.* Vol. 2, *The Colonial and Revolutionary Periods.* San Francisco: Harper and Row, 1983.

Seaver, Paul S. *The Puritan Lectureships: The Politics of Religious Dissent.* Stanford: Stanford University Press, 1970.

Shuckburgh, E. S. *Emmanuel College.* London: T. E. Robinson and Co., 1909.

Shuffleton, Frank Charles. *Thomas Hooker, 1586–1647.* Princeton: Princeton University Press, 1977.

Simpson, Alan. *Puritanism in Old and New England.* Chicago: University of Chicago Press, 1955.

Smith, Harold. *The Ecclesiastical History of Essex.* Colchester, U.K.: Benham and Co., 1932.

Stoever, William K. B. *'A Faire and Easie Way to Heaven': Covenant Theology and Antinomianism in Early Massachusetts.* Middletown, Conn.: Wesleyan University Press, 1978.

Swaim, Kathleen M. "'Come and Hear': Women's Puritan Evidences." In *American Women's Autobiography: Fea(s)ts of Memory,* edited by Margo Culley, 32–56. Madison: University of Wisconsin Press, 1992.

Thompson, Roger. *Women in Stuart England and America, a Comparative Study.* London: Routledge and Kegan Paul, 1974.

Tyacke, Nicholas. *Anti-Calvinists: The Rise of English Arminianism, c. 1590–1640.* Oxford: Clarendon Press, 1987.

Ulrich, Laurel Thatcher. *Goodwives: Image and Reality in the Lives of Women in Northern New England, 1650–1750.* New York: Alfred A. Knopf, 1982.

———. "Vertuous Women Found: New England Ministerial Literature, 1668–1735." In *Women in American Religion,* edited by Janet Wilson James. Philadelphia: University of Pennsylvania Press, 1980.

Wallace, Dewey D., Jr. *Puritans and Predestination: Grace in English Protestant Theology, 1525–1695.* Chapel Hill: University of North Carolina Press, 1982.

Walzer, Michael. *The Revolution of the Saints: A Study in the Origins of Radical Politics.* Cambridge: Harvard University Press, 1965.

Werge, Thomas. *Thomas Shepard.* Boston: Twayne Publishers, 1987.

Williams, George Huntston. "Called by Thy Name, Leave Us Not: The Case of Mrs. Joan Drake, a Formative Episode in the Pastoral Career of Thomas Hooker in England." *Harvard Library Bulletin* 16 (1968): 111–28, 278–303.

———. "Essay 1: The Life of Thomas Hooker in England and Holland, 1586–1633." In *Thomas Hooker: Writings in England and Holland, 1626–1633,* edited by George H. Williams, Norman Pettit, Winfried Herget, and Sargent Bush, Jr. Cambridge: Harvard University Press, 1975.

———. *The Radical Reformation.* Vol. 15, *Sixteenth Century Essays and Studies,* 3d ed., edited by Charles G. Nauert, Jr. Kirksville, Mo.: Sixteenth Century Journal Publishers, 1992.

Wright, C. Conrad. *The Beginnings of Unitarianism in America.* Boston: Starr King Press, 1955.

Ziff, Larz. *The Career of John Cotton, Puritanism and the American Experience.* Princeton: Princeton University Press, 1962.

INDEX